UTOPIA

Consulting Editors

The Editor

GEORGE KATEB is Professor of Political
Science at Amherst College. He graduated Phi
Beta Kappa from Columbia College and received
his A.M. and Ph.D. from Columbia University.
Dr. Kateb is the author of two other books,
Utopia and Its Enemies and *Political Theory:
Its Nature and Uses*. Among his numerous con-
tributions to scholarly publications are several
articles on futurist and utopian thought, including
"On Report from Iron Mountain," "The Political
Thought of Herbert Marcuse," and "The Road
to *1984.*"

UTOPIA

EDITED BY

George Kateb

ATHERTON PRESS

New York 1971

Contents

Introduction   1
GEORGE KATEB

1 : *An Essay on Utopian Possibility*   29
FRANCIS GOLFFING & BARBARA GOLFFING

2 : *Towards More Vivid Utopias*   41
MARGARET MEAD

3 : *Freedom and the Control of Men*   57
B. F. SKINNER

4 : *The Cult of Efficiency*   77
CHRISTOPHER JENCKS

5 : *The Anti-Utopia of the Twentieth Century*   81
EUGEN WEBER

6 : *Utopianism and Politics*   91
J. L. TALMON

7 : *Out of Utopia: Toward a Reorientation*
    of Sociological Analysis   103
RALF DAHRENDORF

8 : *America in the Technetronic Age*   127
ZBIGNIEW BRZEZINSKI

9 : *Robots and Rebels*   151
ARTHUR P. MENDEL

Index   157

Introduction

George Kateb

I

Utopia is a bore. Listen to a great modern poet in one of his most
famous poems:

> There is not any haunt of prophecy,
> Nor any old chimera of the grave,
> Neither the golden underground, nor isle
> Melodius, where spirits gat them home,
> Nor visionary south, nor cloudy palm
> Remote on heaven's hill, that has endured
> As April's green endures; or will endure
> Like her remembrance of awakened birds,
> Or her desire for June and evening, tipped
> By the consummation of the swallow's wings.[1]

It is true that the main play in Wallace Stevens' "Sunday Morning"
is between mortal delight and "some imperishable bliss" after death
and never to come, between consolations that are more than consolations and consolations that are less than nothing. But the poem's
force can be effortlessly directed against visions of the good life on
earth. There is a sweet irony in the phrase, "As April's green en-

1

dures." April's green returns every year; but it appears only to vanish; it is the very symbol of all that is ephemeral, and all the more beautiful for its ephemerality. Being beautiful, it is real, and in its reality it makes the unsubstantial, the longed-for, the imaginary, appear false, unworthy. Like heaven, utopia can be brought under this indictment. Makers of utopias may share the poet's scorn for fantasies of the afterlife. But they do, after all, find life as it is lived grossly insufficient, and dream of what is immeasurably better. April's green is not good enough for them: the idealist imagination must contrive something greener. For their pains, however, they may achieve only the poet's rebuke. The pleasures of the senses must suffice, and do. Imaginary felicity is counterfeit.

Stevens' poem expresses a kind of perennial hostility to utopian aspirations. There is too much in the world, it may be thought, for utopia to compete with. When there is an abundance of things in the world as we know it to sing and praise, why waste time in rejection and in trying to dream up some other world — some other world, furthermore, as unlikely to come as heaven itself? Put away childish things; grow up; accept reality as it is, and the rewards will be great and genuine.

One can easily see that the sentiment behind "Sunday Morning" may be thought callous. It may be fine for a poet reconciled to the world and for his well-fed audience to look down on radical strivings after the good life. But what about the countless millions in their misery? Isn't "April's green" yet one more opiate for their suffering? After all, the speaker in Stevens' poem is obviously a well-favored and privileged woman. She may have her own sufferings; they would be, however, the sufferings that come from surfeit. She not only can afford to indulge in the esthetic attitude, she may even be driven to it by the very fact that all her other appetites are satisfied. If that is the case, well and good. She has reached the point where the cunning of the senses must take over. She must now be artful, so as to be assured pleasures in a world that gives her all that her body needs. She is already in utopia. Her implicit point of view, however, condemns great masses of people to stay outside it.

For them, "April's green" would be a substitute for a decent life, rather than the climax to it. The utopian defender is led to demand that others have the same chances she has had. He is also led to attack all those who would base an anti-utopian outlook on a sentiment like that of Stevens' speaker. Let all mankind also be able to find utopia a bore.

II

If realized, would not then utopia be a cheat? Listen to the French playwright, Eugene Ionesco:

> The "society" I have tried to depict in "The Bald Soprano" is a society that is perfect; I mean where all social problems have been resolved. Unfortunately, this has no effect upon life as it is lived.
>
> The play deals with a world where economic worries are a thing of the past, a universe without mystery, in which everythink runs smoothly for one section of humanity at least. I have no doubt that this is the world of tomorrow....
>
> ...I believe that it is precisely when we see the last of economic problems and class warfare... that we shall also see that this solves nothing, indeed that our problems are only beginning. We can no longer avoid asking ourselves what we are doing here on earth, and how, having no deep sense of our destiny, we can endure the crushing weight of the material world....
>
> The people in "The Bald Soprano" have no hunger, no conscious desires; they are bored stiff. But people who are unconsciously alienated don't even know that they are bored. They feel it vaguely, hence the final explosion — which is quite useless, as the characters and situations are both static and interchangeable, and everything ends where it started.[2]

Ionesco's argument could be filled out by reference to human experience as we already know it. There is abundant testimony in favor of the view that without the existence of many kinds of pain, physical and psychological, pleasure loses its savor. It may even lose its very meaning. It takes little sophistication to ratify what philosophers like Plato and John Stuart Mill say; namely, that for pleasure to be intense, some contrast is needed, some comparison provided by earlier or by anticipated suffering. If utopia means, above everything else, the elimination of suffering, does it not therefore necessarily mean the elimination of the preconditions of pleasure? If that is true, can we not agree with Ionesco, and others, when they suggest that utopia really does not raise the general level of human well-being, but only impoverishes human experience? Is not utopia truly a cheat?

A possible answer is that utopia is worth the risk Ionesco poses. It is worth the risk if pleasure — or at least, intense pleasure — is rejected as a sufficient standard. Whatever the fate of pleasure in a world hypothetically denuded of many or most of the main sources of suffering, some other huge possibility is opened up. It is a possibility just vaguely mentioned by Ionesco, and ignored by others who think like him. It is suggested by two political moralists equal in passion but separate in temperament. I refer to George Orwell and Norman Mailer.

In "Looking Back on the Spanish War," published in 1943, Orwell in a mood of outrage denounces,

> The damned impertinence of these politicians, priests, literary men, and what-not who lecture the working-class socialist for his "materialism"! All that the working man demands is what these others would consider the indispensable minimum without which human life cannot be lived at all. Enough to eat, freedom from the haunting terror of unemployment, the knowledge that your children will get a fair chance, a bath once a day, clean linen reasonably often, a roof that doesn't leak, and short enough working hours to leave you with a little energy when the day is done.[3]

Let us notice that Orwell's imagination does not soar very high. His notion of the good life is largely characterized by the absence of great evils. He really is indifferent to utopian claims when they go beyond the removal of the ancient woes: radical inequality, poverty, discrimination, war, and degrading labor. Indeed, he is hostile to the notion of a life of untroubled ease. In any case, what holds for a more positive utopia, a more ambitious utopia, would also hold for his idealism. The same question can be put to those who dream of Orwell's minimal utopia as well as to those who, in their imagination, crave a good deal more. With great pains gone, would not utopia be a cheat? What Orwell goes on to say after the words quoted above constitutes a kind of answer.

> To raise the standard of living of the whole world to that of Britain would not be a greater undertaking than the war we have just fought. I don't claim, and I don't know who does, that that would solve anything in itself. It is merely that privation and brute labor have to be abolished before the real problems of humanity can be tackled. The major problem of our time is the decay of the belief in personal immortality, and it cannot be dealt with while the average human being is either drudging like an ox or shivering in fear of the secret police.... How right [the working classes] are to realise that the belly comes before the soul, not in the scale of values but in point of time.[4]

The key sentence is: "It is merely that privation and brute labor have to be abolished before the real problems of humanity can be tackled."

For Orwell, the real problems are spiritual. Nothing can give the individual earthly immortality. Nothing readily conceivable can restore the hold of a belief in the afterlife. I assume Orwell did not himself believe in Christian doctrine; and I also assume he would not have wanted any doctrine he thought false to be thought true by others — whatever the utility of the doctrine. Orwell was a liberal. Given these assumptions, it is not clear — Orwell does not indicate — how "the real problems of humanity can be tackled." Obviously there is no *solution*. Death is death. Perhaps the semblance of a solution could be found in a full, rich life: perhaps to complete Orwell's suggestion a more positive utopian aspiration is called for. As Herbert Marcuse puts it in *Eros and Civilization*:

> Death can become a token of freedom. The necessity of death does not refute the possibility of final liberation. Like the other necessities, it can be made rational — painless. Men can die without anxiety if they know that what they love is protected from

misery and oblivion. After a fulfilled life, they may take it
upon themselves to die — at a moment of their own choosing.[5]

If that vision were made real, who then could call utopia a cheat?

In Mailer's novel, *Barbary Shore* (1951), we can find another
attitude to use in trying to come to terms with Ionesco's comments.
One of the characters (McLeod) says:

> I must admit that in the past the sight of a house in the suburb
> of some city or other was enough to depress me with that damn
> afernoon sunlight and the shingles in *kitsch* and all the bloody
> papamamas with their brat in the baby carriage. To anyone who
> attempts to change the world, that's the specter. Subjectively,
> there's always the fear: that's where I end up. And objectively
> it's even worse, for you know that the end product of your la-
> bors, if you are successful, is that the multi-millions in misery
> will graduate only to that, and the brotherhood of man is a
> world of stinking baby carriages. It's the paradox of the revo-
> lutionary who seeks to create a world in which he would find it
> intolerable to live.[6]

For a moment, McLeod sounds like those "politicians, priests, literary men, and what-not" whom Orwell attacked for their hypocrisy
and insensitivity. To be sure, behind McLeod's words is a complexity
Orwell would not have granted to the types he chastised. McLeod
does not stop:

> You might say the human function of socialism . . . is to raise
> mankind to a higher level of suffering, for given the hypothesis
> that man has certain tragic confrontations, the alternative is
> between a hungry belly and a hungry mind, but fulfillment there
> is never.[7]

"Fulfillment there is never"; but some ways of suffering are
better than others. They are more purely human, less animal, more
dignified — it is not very easy to designate them. With McLeod's
utterance, Mailer goes beyond Marcuse: not even the good life can
quiet the mind, even if we leave the consideration of death to one
side. He in effect rejects Marx's eighth thesis on Feuerbach: "So-

cial life is essentially *practical*. All mysteries which mislead theory to mysticism find their rational solution in human practice and in the comprehension of this practice." On the contrary, the best social reality cannot satisfy or exhaust all the urgings of mind.[8] However, at least something can be gained, some increase in the decency of the human condition can be gained. Could utopia then still rightly be called a cheat?

III

So far we have seen that some think utopian life would be false or flat. Others add that utopia is a corpse. Listen to a prominent German sociologist (from an essay reprinted below):

> The difference between utopia and a cemetery is that occasionally some things do happen in utopia.... But ... all processes going on in utopian societies follow recurrent patterns and occur within, and as part of, the design of the whole.... Although some of its parts are moving in predetermined, calculable ways, utopia as a whole remains a *perpetuum immobile*.[9]

Dahrendorf points to a recurrent feature in utopian thought, the fixed and uneventful quality of life pictured in it. It is true that unhappiness is far more interesting to write about and read about than is happiness. So much of the world's literature dwells on human misfortune and wrongdoing; it dwells on human action in the face of peril, limitation, scarcity, necessity, strife. These latter seem to constitute the sources of change in human life. There may be regular patterns into which the many kinds of unhappiness fall; but patterns or not, the surface of reality, throughout time, affords an overpowering spectacle of mutability. We read about it compulsively, in endless fascination, horrified but enchanted. Next to this record, the story of life in the famous utopias is truly static; it is insulting to the imagination. One of the greatest of all utopian writers — perhaps the greatest after Plato — was ready to acknowledge the fact. In *A Modern Utopia* (1905), H. G. Wells said:

There must always be a certain effect of hardness and thinness about Utopian speculations. Their common fault is to be comprehensively jejune. That which is the blood and warmth and reality of life is largely absent; there are no individualities, but only generalised people. In almost every Utopia — except, perhaps, Morris's "News from Nowhere" — one sees handsome but characterless buildings, symmetrical and perfect cultivations, and a multitude of people, healthy, happy, beautifully dressed, but without personal distinction whatever.[10]

But it would be wrong to think that the complaint voiced by Dahrendorf, by Wells, and by others is simply an esthetic one. There are traces of estheticism — that cannot be denied. There may even be a certain hardheartedness in insisting that utopia is bad because to a reader it is uninteresting: to praise life as interesting is often to forget the suffering of others that has gone into making it interesting. Nevertheless, more is at issue. That is the apparent incompatibility between the intention of most utopian writers and the inevitability and moral desirability of change. It is right to say that almost all utopian designs do not reckon with change. The common assumption is that once the design is realized in the world — if it ever is — it will continue indefinitely in the form in which it began. Utopian thought is dominated by a "rage for order." A strong utopian impetus is to save the world from as much of its confusion and disorder as possible. Utopia is a dream of order, of quiet and calm. Its background is the nightmare of history. At the same time, the order, in each case, is thought to be either perfect or as close to perfect as human affairs can get. How, in truth, could a thinker, possessed both of a rage for order and a sense that he commands a vision of perfection (or near perfection) comfortably allow for change? By his lights, change is the very sign of imperfection; change must always be a symptom of unhappiness. And, by definition, change away from perfection must necessarily be for the worse. To build in the possibility for change in utopia, therefore, is to compromise the usual premises of utopian thought.

Against this frame of mind critics of utopia direct some of their fiercest reproaches. But it must be noted that in the utopian tradition itself, one writer at least — again it is Wells — has tried to break with the usual premises. He says at the beginning of the first chapter of *A Modern Utopia:*

> The Utopia of a modern dreamer must needs differ in one fundamental aspect from the Nowheres and Utopias men planned before Darwin quickened the thought of the world. Those were all perfect and static States, a balance of happiness won for ever against the forces of unrest and disorder that inhere in things. One beheld a healthy and simple generation enjoying the fruits of the earth in an atmosphere of virtue and happiness, to be followed by other virtuous, happy, and entirely similar generations, until the Gods grew weary.... But the Modern Utopia must not be static but kinetic, must shape not as a permanent state but as a hopeful stage, leading to a long ascent of stages.[11]

But Wells is an exception. Even he did not always follow this instinct in his other utopian writing. Indeed, he really does not explore the ways of institutionalizing change — social change — in *A Modern Utopia.*

In any case, the critics of utopia assert the ineluctability of the facts of life, which facts can be subsumed under such categories as human restlessness, the desire for novelty, the need to adapt to the unforeseen, the emergence of discoveries and inventions, the limits of predictability, the growth of mind, the disclosure of new possibilities and opportunities, the dialectic of style, and so on. To be sure, efforts can be made to stifle these things. But then the distinction between utopia and totalitarianism is blurred; that between utopia and a land of incomplete people may be lost altogether. Aldous Huxley's *Brave New World* demonstrates this point with a justly famous power. Eugen Weber, in an article reprinted below, summarizes the matter:

> Insofar as the anti-utopian allows us a glimmer of hope, it lies in the instincts, in fantasy, in the irrational, in the peculiarly individualistic and egotistic characteristics most likely to shatter any system or order. This accounts for the importance of basic feelings — sex, love, selfishness, fantasy — which all utopian planners try to control and in which all anti-utopians seem to put their faith, insofar as they have any faith. Again and again,

like Ray Bradbury in his remarkable short story, *Usher II,* the anti-utopian calls on the irrational to disrupt and destroy the planned order.[12]

J. L. Talmon, in a lecture reprinted below, is even more severe:

Utopianism postulates free self-expression by the individual and at the same time absolute social cohesion. This combination is possible only if all individuals agree. All individuals, however, do not agree. Therefore, if you expect unanimity, there is ultimately no escape from dictatorship. The individual must either be forced to agree, or his agreement must be engineered by some kind of fake plebiscite, or he must be treated as an outlaw, or traitor, or counterrevolutionary subversive, or whatever you will.[13]

Fearful of change, the utopian planner may reduce life to a frightful simplicity in order to remove all things that tempt or lead people into desiring or imagining contrasts and alternatives. Manipulation may manifest itself in many ways in the supposed name of human happiness. Worse, if these methods fail, the totalitarian threat to which Talmon refers may materialize though disguised.

There are thus several lessons modern utopianism must learn — lessons incredibly hard for anyone who is serious about, and sympathetic with, the idea of utopia. These lessons are that no social arrangement can be perfect; that not all movements for change can be attributed to human weakness or sinfulness; that change can sometimes be for the better; and that to try to prevent change probably is not only foolhardy but also likely to require such stratagems and devices as to compromise the premises of utopian thought far more seriously than allowing for change, in the first place. These lessons are especially appropriate in modern times because the growth in scientific knowledge and technical capacity constantly disturbs life in society, offering not only threats, not only cures to ills science itself creates, but also promises of felicity. This is not to preach a doctrine of inevitable progress; it is only to reckon with the commonplace. On this matter, Wells gives the lead to his fellow-utopians.

Is there nothing to be said on the other side? Do the inevitability of change in circumstances other than inhumanly repressive (or primitive), and the moral desirability of some change, destroy the idea of utopia? They may. But then they may not. If utopia is to survive this consideration, it must be possible to conceive of a situation in which free thought, spontaneous life, meaningful choices, the eruption of the unexpected, the presence of the mysterious, are all compatible with a way of life which could still be thought utopian. The heart of the matter, in my opinion, is virtue. That is, can we imagine that throughout the processes of change, men would remain committed to preserving the fundamental principles of utopian society? Though thought, research, inquiry remain free, would utopian citizens still shrink from applying the results of free thought, research, and inquiry in evil ways? Though imagination roams where it wants, would utopian citizens be able to continue uninfected by the impulses to enact in reality, and in a literal manner, the wild or unholy deeds sometimes prompted by imagination? Though speculation is encouraged, would utopian citizens withstand the charms of skepticism or intellectual perversity enough to stay loyal to their principles? Does a thorough training in virtue — if there is such a thing — kill what we now think of as genuinely spontaneous behavior? Or is training in virtue, if it is to meet utopian expectations, really more like conditioning or programming than it is like education and cultivation? If it is expected that all choices, though free, are nevertheless virtuous — simply or ambiguously — would a sufficiently large range of human conduct be preserved by utopian society? In the face of the eruption of the unexpected, would utopian citizens keep their balance and hold on to their principles? In the face of the mysterious, would utopian citizens want to stay happy? In short, can utopia be recognizable as life, but better than the life we know?

These question are abstract, unreal. They may not even be put properly. Correspondingly, the answers to them do not exist. There can only be sketches of answers. The entire subject, as befits utopia, is tentative. We can do nothing more than point to it, not sure that we point in the right direction. Nevertheless we cling to the notion, as old as Plato, but easily lost sight of, that virtue is the key to the persistence of a utopian way of life, and that, in turn, the key to virtue is education in the fullest sense. In modern times, the main systematic joining of education, virtue, and utopia is found in the work of the psychologist B. F. Skinner. Especially in *Walden Two* (1948), and in an essay reprinted below, "Freedom and the Control of Men" (1955), Skinner outlines the educational practices needed to sustain his utopia.[14] More than that, he writes with sufficient generality and awareness to suggest the kinds of questions any utopian writer must ponder, even if Skinner's utopia, in part or as a whole, is rejected.

Rejected, in part or as a whole, Skinner's utopia has been, by almost everyone who has written on it.[15] He has a great capacity to excite animus. In his utopian novel, *Walden Two,* he puts these awful words in the mouth of Frazier, the creator of the utopian colony:

> I deny that freedom exists at all. I must deny it — or my program would be absurd. You can't have a science about a subject matter which hops capriciously about. Perhaps we can never *prove* that man isn't free; it's an assumption. But the increasing success of a science of behavior makes it more and more plausible.[16]

Skinner's thought is dominated by an attitude toward human freedom that is always hostile, and usually careless in its philosophical handling. He seems to go out of his way to say or suggest that freedom is only another name for behavior not understood by the actor or the observer; that freedom is normally expressed as madness, impulse, or disobedience; that the sense of being free is compatible with *any* kind of relation between a man and his society; that improvement in educating the young will be accompanied by a reduction in the ability of the adult to engage in unpredictable, unforeseen activity; and that the idea of freedom can be dismissed when education for virtue is discussed. It is no wonder that Skinner has enemies. There is a touch of the mad manipulator in him that comes out now and then — which is to say, too often.

He is also heedless and abrupt in his comments on democracy. Walden Two is, in its political arrangements, elitist. Effort is made to show that it is a largely unpolitical community, that its way of life can dispense with most of what is included in politics, and that the control that remains is safely left in the hands of its creator and his few associates. Skinner assumes that the success of his enterprise requires the end of democratic government. He breezes past all the perils of his position in sentences like these:

> All governments make certain forms of punishment contingent upon certain kinds of acts. In democratic countries these contingencies are expressed by the notion of responsible choice. But the notion may have no meaning under governmental practices formulated in other ways and would certainly have no place in systems which did not use punishment.[17]

> No matter how effective we judge current democratic practices to be, how highly we value them or how long we expect them to survive, they are almost certainly not the *final* form of government.[18]

Skinner is too eager to reach the point at which it could be said that democracy had to give way to another form: his form.

He is also indifferent to some of the force behind the charges that the way of life he proposes is thin, sterile, lifeless, ridiculously confined. It is not only that the inhabitants of Walden Two seem to one critic to be "zombies,"[19] and to another "sheep,"[20] it is also that, to put it more kindly, they seem dull to contemplate. They lead a life it would be dull to lead. One can make this judgment and still be free of any excessive romanticism. The inhabitants are plain and nice. They work well, and like to listen to serious music. They are polite enough; they are devoid of harshness and fanaticism. They really are not like Mao's new men. But they have no spirit, no spirituality. They have no disguises, no indirectness, no play. It is impossibly to imagine them sarcastic, even ironic. Their jests are not funny. One cannot believe them capable of uttering an interesting sentence, or of wanting to utter one. If the quality of speech, of consciousness, is the final standard by which to judge a culture, then Skinner's utopia is a failure. His creatures have no inner life. They are two-dimensional, not because Skinner is a bad novelist, but because he is a narrow moral psychologist. His creatures are inferior to the people we know or read about, not just inferior to the people we want to see come into existence. They are nothing to be proud of, nothing to populate an imaginary world with. They are not even civilized.

Having said all this, we must conclude that in the substance of his teaching, Skinner does not project a utopian way of life in which education works for a virtue that is satisfactorily full, a virtue that is meant to be exercised in a complicated, demanding, surprising, and changing world. (We leave aside the criticisms that have been or could be made against Skinner's educational techniques on the grounds that they produce not education but conditioning and manipulation.) Why then praise him?

For several reasons. First, he encourages us to believe — though without actually proving the point — that, within somewhat broader limits than common sense allows, human beings can be deliberately trained to a certain way of life, to become what those who train them want them to become. The plain fact is that all cultures have some sense of this kind of purposiveness, some sense of education as training, as initiation, as "acculturation." It is just about impossible to think of a culture without this sense. Skinner faces this fact honestly. And despite the almost unseemly pleasure he sometimes takes in the idea of the plasticity of human nature, he is surely right in scorning those who are appalled by it.

Second, almost without intending it, he encourages us — again without proving anything — probably this is not a matter of proof but of very tentative disposition — he encourages us to hope that the mortally serious doctrine of original sin may not be quite as debilitating to utopia as many would like to believe, and as others fear they have to believe. With the world as it is, and as it has always been, perhaps only a fool — and a zealous one, at that — can fail to believe in original sin. (No theology is needed to support the belief, just a moment's thought.) Skinner does believe, however, that *under proper circumstances,* and only those, pride, the most encompassing sin, and the sin that fathers the other sins, can be dealt with. It can be effaced, or transmuted, or neutralized, by the right education, begun early enough, and then sustained by an entire way of life. He believes that all the desired moral behavior can be prepared for. He also believes that the role of punishment, deprivation, frustration, the role of forbidding, threatening, and repressing can be substantially reduced, if not eliminated altogether. To be sure, his optimism is too high; and the social life he conceives, in order to make his optimism plausible, much too simple. "Positive reinforcement" can do just so much: it is not sufficient as a basis for civilized behavior. But he does give a lead others can follow. He keeps one of the great ideas of the Enlightenment alive.

Third, he restores the twofold Platonic conception: without education no great social ideals are realizable, and that by "education" is meant not only formal schooling but also the contribution made to the growing child's character by all he encounters, experiences, all that surrounds him and impresses itself on him, often without his knowing it. Skinner, as we have said, founds his utopian idealism on the treatment of the child. In this regard, he is unlike two of the most influential idealist thinkers, Herbert Marcuse and Norman O. Brown. Both these thinkers, far more daring, truly more beautiful in their imaginative flights, pay no attention to the education of the young. They sketch in, tantalizingly, the finished society. They talk about some of its psychological and economic presuppositions and accompaniments. They talk about its rewards. But they do not go to the root, the child. Skinner does. That is one aspect. On the other, in his extended sense of "education," he is aware that there is very little, if anything, that is innocent of importance to the formation of character. Obviously, it is easier to deal with this consideration when the locus of idealism is a small community, as in the case of Skinner. It may be that that is the only situation in which it is at all possible to deal with it. Smallness facilitates control. Whatever the case, however, Skinner gives centrality to this simple idea — a simple idea, but one frequently ignored, and also one that must give pause to any utopian writer whose social system is not the small community.

Last, Skinner tries to come to terms with the question of the relation between the formation of character and the institution of the family. Far as he is from Freud and the Freudians in almost all his thought, he ponders the consequences for character of the nuclear family (in Chapter 17 of *Walden Two*). So much of the human condition is determined by the fact that we are not born adults, but are formed in darkness and unknowing; and by the fact that we have parents, but not of our choosing. (Only Adam and Eve were spared that fate.) Skinner is certainly not the first to include these matters as intrinsic to utopian thought: as always Plato was first. He is not as radical as Plato: as always Plato is the most radical. He is not alone, in modern times, in having designs on orthodox family life, in the name of utopia: one thinks, for example, of Fourier, and of the Oneida community. Still, Skinner makes the effort, brief and insufficiently worked out though it may be.

For all these reasons, then, Skinner should earn our praise. What we cannot praise him for, however, is having achieved even a provisional solution to the prime question: Can virtue supply the basis for reconciling change and utopia?

IV

But suppose some resolution or other were possible, how much would be gained? We have hypothetically set quite strict confinements on the sorts of change the idea of utopia could permit. To some, these confinements are *unacceptably* strict for many reasons, but especially for one: utopia does not allow the heights and depths of human possibility to be reached. Not only is it a bore or a cheat or a corpse. Not only does it seem to preclude intensity of pleasure, and seem to leave the profoundest questions of life untouched, and seem to try madly to chain up change. It does something else, as bad as any of these, or worse. It wars on the idea of heroism. Utopia is unmanly. Listen to the Savage, the deviant in Huxley's *Brave New World:*

I'm claiming the right to be unhappy.... Not to mention the right to grow old and ugly and impotent; the right to have syphilis and cancer; the right to have too little to eat; the right to be lousy; the right to live in constant apprehension of what may happen tomorrow; the right to catch typhoid; the right to be tortured by unspeakable pains of every kind.[21]

The Savage's tone is adolescent. The experiences he craves are all experiences the desire for which would vanish in the attainment. Huxley drives him far to make his point about the unspeakable safety of Brave New World. (See the remarks by Christopher Jencks, reprinted below.) Make such allowances for the speech, and you are then prepared to see in it a simpleminded statement that can serve as a reminder of a great theme, the fate of courage in a utopian world. The fate of courage is the key to the quality of manhood. Courage, of course, not confined to feats of war or endurance, but for tests, trials, challenges, contests of every kind, with oneself or others or nature, bloodless but manly. How could utopia find room for them?

Plato had to find room for them, at least for those that are inherent in war. Fourier delighted in finding room for all but those inherent in war. But twentieth-century utopianism? Wells, it is true, tries to accommodate the adventurous and questing natures. Perhaps he does dispose of the question as satisfactorily as it can be: many kinds of courage are to flourish except for the kind which war favors: the risk of humanly inflicted violent death. Wells took with utmost seriousness (especially in *A Modern Utopia*) the dangers posed by utopian life, the dangers of passivity, softness, the attempt to conceal human promptings toward risk, uncertainty, the gamble. It may very well be that no way of life, not even that of modern utopia, could possibly eliminate these things. They may be, they probably are, inseparable from life itself, though life proceeds in a manner that could be called "utopian." Whether that is true or not, the nagging fact is that the utopian impulse is away from heroism, in the largest understanding of the word. There is almost aversion to it. It is this aversion that deserves to be worried about.

Skinner tries, however, to dispose of the issue. He says:

> Up to 1956 men had been admired, if at all, either for causing
> trouble or alleviating it.... We may mourn the passing of heroes
> but not the conditions which make for heroism. We can spare
> the self-made saint or sage as we spare the laundress on the
> river's bank struggling against fearful odds to achieve clean-
> liness.[22]

But how effective is this remark? The equation of the saint and
sage with the laundress is specious. The standard in the case of
laundry is simple, and easily applied: to get the laundry done as
efficiently as possible, with the smallest amount of annoyance and
drudgery. There are no values inherent in doing the job of laundry;
for almost all people there are no satisfactions gained from it. It
is only a matter of securing the proper means for a banal necessity.
Can we adopt, however, such a narrowly utilitarian scheme when
we think about the range of activities in which courage figures? I do
not think so. Of course, courage, like other virtues, is often wel-
comed precisely for its utilitarian advantages: it is instrumental to
victory over oneself or others. Doubtless it would not have received
the praise it always has were it not so intimately a part of success
in struggles of one kind or another. But that is not the end of the
story. A good case could be made out for the view that apart from
its *practical* utility, courage, like other virtues and human qualities,
is worthy. How is it valuable? It is valuable because it shows what
people are capable of; it permits people to display themselves significantly; it is a major link between people and a public world as it
is a major link between a man and his innermost recesses; it is the
source of the most important kinds of the sense of achievement; it
confers value on attainments that would, if easily had, possess no
savor; it saves the world from boredom, if allowed expression; it
leads to honor and a reputation for magnanimity, the desire for
which is not ignominious. "[C]ausing trouble or alleviating it" does
not exhaust the concept of heroism, as Skinner thinks. Courage is
thus instrumental in ways Skinner does not perceive. Sages and
saints are not laundresses. War, scarcity, and malign circumstance
can be eliminated, and courage still demand and deserve a place in
the moral structure of the world.

But notice what Skinner has done by writing as he has. He and others in the utopian tradition force on their critics the tremendous task of re-examining that moral structure, and of defending what has hitherto been taken for granted. (It is not only the utopian assault on courage that is involved, but its assault on many other things as well.) What, then, are those habits, practices, characteristics, situations, in the real world which are truly incompatible with the modern utopian ideal, but which nevertheless can be prized and justified by humane criteria? Let them be identified. Let it be shown — if it can — that these things can exist only if the utopian ideal is attenuated. (Surely we do not want to say "only if the utopian ideal is abandoned.") It may very well be that the world has been merely enduring or putting up with things that are in fact instrumental (not in a narrow practical sense) to much that is precious. So precious that the utopian tradition stands convicted of anti-humanism when it seeks to remove their preconditions. But the case has to be made, and made without either hysteria or a disguised but callous disregard of human welfare. The full cost of these precious things must be made clear, if the necessity for paying that cost is to be established. There is a cost, for example, in accommodating courage, no matter how splendid the things it engenders. At the least, the utopian tradition can make us look at the real world with new eyes. It can incite moralists to take inventory.

V

Should utopian thought be content with only urging moralists on in the endeavor of inventory? Is its function primarily to goad and criticize, to make society more aware of itself in its "costs and benefits"? Some have said or would say, Yes. If taken too seriously, if taken literally, utopia is illusion. Listen to the words of Marx and Engels:

> The significance of Critical-Utopian Socialism and Communism bears an inverse relation to historical development. In proportion

as the modern class struggle develops and takes definite shape, this fantastic standing apart from the contest, these fantastic attacks on it, lose all practical value and all theoretical justification. Therefore, although the originators of these systems were, in many respects, revolutionary, their disciples have, in every case, formed mere reactionary sects. They hold fast by the original views of their masters, in opposition to the progressive historical development of the proletariat.... They still dream of experimental realisation of their social Utopias, of founding isolated *"phalanstères,"* of establishing "Home Colonies," of setting up a "little Icaria" — duodecimo editions of the New Jerusalem....[23]

In contrast to what is utopia an illusion? Reality, of course. But for Marx and the Marxists, it is not reality considered as a fixed and excellent quantity, in contrast to which utopia is a silly illusion. Rather it is the movement of reality, the movement of history before which all perfectionist speculation, hatched by well-meaning thinkers in isolation, is foolish. History is pregnant with new forms of life which revolution will deliver. These new forms emerge from the old ones, they grow out of them. There is a logic to human development. In the revolutionary act of destroying the old forms, the new ones will gradually come into being. A self-conscious revolutionary class will learn by doing, and will do that which is historically appropriate. This class does not need instruction from idle philosophers. Class consciousness is, by and large, adequate to its historical tasks. This view is the one in which Marx and the Marxists took the greatest pride: it registered the difference between socialism utopian and socialism scientific. It is, finally, science that brands utopia an illusion.

Recently, another scientific version of historicism has arisen. This time, it is based on the trends of technology in the advanced countries of the world, especially the United States. It does not contain a direct attack on utopian thought. Indeed it often seems to be a continuation of it. In the words of Zbigniew Brzezinski (from an article reprinted below) :

A profound change in the intellectual community itself is inherent in this development [the appearance of "politician intel-

lectuals"]. The largely humanist-oriented, occasionally ideologically-minded intellectual-dissenter, who saw his role largely in
terms of proffering social critiques, is rapidly being displaced
either by experts and specialists, who become involved in special governmental undertakings, or by the generalists-integrators,
who become in effect house-ideologues for those in power, providing over-all intellectual integration for disparate actions. A
community of organization-oriented, application-minded intellectuals, relating itself more effectively to the political system
than their predecessors, serves to introduce into the political
system concerns broader than those likely to be generated by that
system itself and perhaps more relevant than those articulated by
outside critics.[24]

We are once again told to bend with the times. If Marx saw in class
violence the method by which historical rationality is brought into
the world, Brzezinski sees in the conscious application of technical-
scientific rationality by an intellectual elite the method by which the
ambiguous promises of modern knowledge are to be made good. In
both specimens of historicist thought, the scope granted to the
freely-ranging, critical, and perfectionist mind — that is, to the
utopian mind — is tiny. But where Marx's prophecy failed in the
Western world only to become a utopian doctrine elsewhere, Brzezinski's combination of muted hope and tentative prognostication
may, in the long run, have more going for it. Furthermore, in both
specimens, the lesson is quite clear: the utopian effort of imagination is non-science to the point of nonsense. It is out of touch with
reality. It wastes on intellectual fabrication energies that should be
put at the disposal of action. In any case, action there will be,
action that will deliver the goods, real goods, goods already implicit
in contemporary tendencies in the real world. Thus, utopia is an
illusion.

Against such historicism, two kinds of objection can be raised.
(We shall speak here only of the recent historicism.) First, there
can be deep skepticism concerning the ability to forecast the future,
even roughly. If utopian thought has been traditionally charged with
simplification because it wants to crowd a world into an image, then
the technical-scientific ideology (and ideology it is) can be charged

with an unwarranted confidence in its powers to describe the future. It is true that some of these ideologists, like Daniel Bell, can warn against the pitfalls of prediction, and enter numerous words of caution about the treacherousness of projecting present tendencies. It is also true that it will not do to scorn the effort to think about what the world may look like twenty or forty years hence, barring the eruption of unimaginable — literally unimaginable — novelties. There are so many novelties *now* in the world, novel problems and novel capacities, that it is legitimate to see our condition as, in many respects, discontinuous with previous experience. If that is so, the temptation is irresistible to look close at what has been happening and to ponder what may happen. It is only when the tone of the futurist ideologists turns imperious — and Brzezinski's sometimes does — that the hackles are right to rise.

Second, there can be revulsion at the substance of the predicted social order. The article by Arthur P. Mendel, parts of which are reprinted below, expresses that revulsion most forcefully, and does so in the name of a humanism to which Brzezinski condescends.[25] Now, Mendel's humanism is not of the utopian variety: it is not the imagination of perfection which Mendel advocates. He too finds his salvation in the real world, though in aspects alien to Brzezinski. And one friendly to the utopian enterprise would probably take satisfaction in Mendel's attack. The point is, however, that the forces for which both men speak, adversary as they are, conspire to eclipse utopia.

To put it plainly, the world we live in is too interesting. Not only in Wallace Stevens' sense: in that sense the world has always been too interesting to those who could afford to observe it from a distance or sample its pleasures. In that sense, the world has always been too interesting for utopia to matter much, except (in Keats' words) to:

...those to whom the miseries of the world
Are misery, and will not let them rest.

No, the world is too interesting in another sense. We have already referred to its novel problems and novel capacities. An entire issue of the journal *Daedalus (Toward the Year 2000: Work in Progress)* is devoted to canvassing them.[26] On the one hand, technology releases magical potencies; all sorts of new sensory experiences are made available; the universe is opened to exploration; many impulses find new modes of discharge; new tastes come into being as hints of felicity are caught; the surface of life undergoes fast and frequent change, and thereby pleases or depresses, but at least stimulates, the lust of the eye; the world becomes for some, in W. H. Auden's phrase, a "limestone landscape," a plastic thing able to be shaped in endlessly various ways. On the other hand, everything increases in scale; the numbers of people wildly multiply; cancer becomes the metaphor of life; the environment is desecrated; natural resources are threatened with exhaustion; the bases of privacy are eroded; the workings of government are shrouded more and more in mystery and secrecy; individuality is suffocated by bureaucracy, community, or fraternity; the weapons of destruction are total; the governors of the world seem impervious to the meaning of what they do, what they threaten to do, what they are capable of doing. Things get better; things get worse; things get better as they get worse; things get worse because they get better.[27] Everything gets publicized, and we are left dazed by the intolerable but absolutely bewitching flow of communication.

What chance has the utopian imagination against all this? Who can bear to follow the windings of the solitary utopian thinker when the world crowds in on one so? But we must, because we must have vision. We must have as full an exploration of possibilities as the inspired thinker can give us. Finally, it is vision that counts, the vision of men who refuse to be violated by novel problems and novel capacities, and who instead try to leap outside their time in order to catch hold of their time. Vision need not be embodied in novels, romances, descriptions of whole imaginary societies. These literary techniques may now in fact be inappropriate to utopian requirements, however well they may once have served. Our present utopian needs are probably best met by philosophical writing which is straight-forwardly unfictional, but imaginative nevertheless. On the other hand, our needs will not be met by blueprints, by schemes too

"Social Criticism and Illusions of the Open Society," *The Massachusetts Review,* X (Spring 1969), 247-279.

24. Zbigniew Brzezinski, "America in the Technetronic Age," *Encounter,* XXX (January 1968), 22. See also Brzezinski's "Revolution and Counterrevolution," *The New Republic,* 158 (June 1, 1968), 23-25.

25. See also John McDermott, "Technology: The Opiate of the Intellectuals," *The New York Review of Books,* XIII (July 31, 1969), 25-35.

26. *Daedalus,* 96 (Summer 1967). See also Robert Boguslaw, *The New Utopians* (Englewood Cliffs, N.J.: Prentice-Hall, 1965); Herman Kahn and Anthony J. Wiener, *The Year 2000* (New York: Macmillan, 1967); Donald N. Michael, *The Unprepared Society* (New York: Basic Books, 1968); and Daniel Bell, "Notes on the Post-industrial Society," I and II, *The Public Interest,* no. 6 (Winter 1967), pp. 24-35, and no. 7 (Spring 1967), pp. 102-118.

27. See Norman Mailer, *Cannibals and Christians* (New York: Dial Press, 1966), p. 4.

28. This point dominates the most impressive work by Fred L. Polak, *The Image of the Future,* trans. by Elise Boulding (2 vols., New York: Oceana, 1961).

FOR FURTHER READING

This selective list is meant to supplement the citations in the Introduction.

Boulding, Kenneth E. *The Meaning of the Twentieth Century.* New York: Harper & Row, 1964.

Brown, Norman O. *Love's Body.* New York: Random House, 1966.

Buber, Martin. *Paths in Utopia.* New York: Macmillan, 1950.

Cohn, Norman. *The Pursuit of the Millennium.* London: Secker & Warburg, 1957.

Dostoyevsky, Fyodor. *Notes from Underground.* Trans. by Constance Garnett. Many editions.

Doxiades, Constantinos A. *Between Dystopia and Utopia.* Hartford, Conn.: Trinity College Press, 1966.

Ferkiss, Victor C. *Technological Man.* New York: George Braziller, 1969.

Forster, E. M. "The Machine Stops," in *The Eternal Moment and Other Stories.* London: Sidgwick & Jackson, 1928.

Golffing, Francis. "Notes towards a Utopia," *The Partisan Review,* XXVII (Summer 1960), 514-525.

Hillegas, Mark R. *The Future as Nightmare: H. G. Wells and the Anti-utopians.* New York: Oxford University Press, 1967.

Horsburgh, H. J. N. "The Relevance of the Utopian," *Ethics,* LXVII (January 1954), 127-138.

James, William. "Remarks at the Peace Banquet," in *Memories and Studies.* New York: Longmans, Green, 1911.

James, William. "The Moral Equivalent of War," in *Essays on Faith and Morals.* New York: Longmans, Green, 1947.

Lenin, V. I. *State and Revolution.* New York: International Publishers, 1932.

Lippmann, Walter. *The Good Society.* New York: Grosset's Universal Library, 1956.

Mannheim, Karl. *Ideology and Utopia.* Trans. by L. Wirth and E. Shils. New York: Harvest Books, n.d.

Manuel, Frank E., ed. *Utopias and Utopian Thought.* Boston: Houghton Mifflin, 1966.

Marcuse, Herbert. *One-Dimensional Man.* Boston: Beacon, 1964.

Marcuse, Herbert. *An Essay on Liberation.* Boston: Beacon, 1969.

Mead, Margaret. "The Future as the Basis for Establishing a Shared Culture," *Daedalus,* 94 (Winter 1965), 135-155.

Moore, Barrington, Jr. *Political Power and Social Theory: Seven Studies*. New York: Harper Torchbooks, 1965.

Mumford, Lewis. *The Transformations of Man*. New York: Harper, 1956.

Negley, Glenn, and J. Max Patrick. *The Quest for Utopia*. New York: H. Schuman, 1952.

Orwell, George. *The Road to Wigan Pier*. New York: Harcourt, Brace and World, 1958.

Popper, Karl. *The Open Society and Its Enemies*. Princeton: Princeton University Press, 1950.

Russell, Bertrand. *Proposed Roads to Freedom*. London: G. Allen, 1918.

Seidenberg, Roderick. *Post-Historic Man*. Chapel Hill, N.C.: University of North Carolina Press, 1950.

Shklar, Judith N. *After Utopia*. Princeton: Princeton University Press, 1957.

Walsh, Chad. *From Utopia to Nightmare*. New York: Harper & Row, 1962.

Young, Michael. *The Rise of the Meritocracy*. New York: Random House, 1959.

Zamiatin, Eugene. *We*. Trans. by Gregory Zilboorg. New York: Dutton, 1924.

1: *An Essay on Utopian Possibility*

Francis Golffing
Barbara Golffing

The idea of Utopia is timeless. That is to say, it does not develop historically; the earliest Utopias are no less advanced than the latest. However, the idea requires to be restated in terms relevant to each new period of history; and to this extent every Utopia is an historic act: part of the continuum we call man's evolution.

I

All writers of Utopias (be they novelists, social planners, or "mere" philosophers) necessarily come up against certain crucial questions which they must answer, either publicly or in their own minds. Chief among these questions are: what is possible to the human animal, in strictly operational terms, and what is desirable for the welfare of man, both individually and collectively? Evidently there is no obvious

From *The Centennial Review*, vol. 7, no. 4 (Fall 1963), pp. 470-480.

correlation, sanctioned by tradition, between these two lines of inquiry; yet the Utopist finds himself under the obligation of treating them as complementary aspects of one and the same question — Tolstoi's great question: "What does man live for?" He must do this in face of the fact, as obvious to him as it is to everyone else, that human history teems with undesirable possibilities and impossible desiderata. These contradictory combinations he too must, and will, *record* while refusing to view them as necessary features of human development. While most observers accept them as given — part and parcel of man's condition, or man's essential paradox — he believes such combinations to be freakish, their components to be capable of final disassociation, not only verbally or logically, but in terms of actual operation, human behavior. It is this, and nothing else, that sets him apart from his non-utopian fellows.

In short, the cardinal issue — what does the species essentially want and what is it fit to accomplish? — is capable of solution, he thinks; and that solution leaves ample room for human striving, competition, and dissent. But there is no place in it either for impossible desires or for achievements that are possible, yet unwanted. Whatever is dictated by man's biosocial needs is capable of ultimate satisfaction, provided he creates the conditions necessary to such process. And whatever runs counter to these needs he can keep from happening, by the same token and in the same manner, the only bars being, in either case, "crass casualty" (i.e., sheer accident) and biological exhaustion.

As a matter of fact, most Utopists of the past (and present) have dodged the central issue in one way or another, and to the extent that they have done this have failed to live up to their noble calling. Not from cowardice, surely, but from a commendable sense of "hard facts" — facts which they felt had to be either stoically accepted or else *frankly* escaped from. William Morris, in his admirable utopian romances, well illustrates the latter procedure. Morris looked technology in the face, and then left it on one side, taking the opposite direction. Nobody can accuse him of having been blind to the inevitability of technical progress; yet his look — which was close, not at all casual — convinced him that this way lay perdition and not, as most of his contemporaries would have it, salvation. All the same, in a deeper sense Morris may be said to have dodged the issue, which is not between hand labor and machine labor, or between socialism and capitalism, but between two basic cultural temptations: toward productiveness on the one hand, and toward destruction on the other. These temptations have been at war in *homo sapiens* since the beginning of culture and must have been experienced by the primitive toolmaker or tribal chief quite as forcibly as they are by today's engineer or political leader.

Take, on the other hand, a writer like Sir Thomas More, who for all his contempt of hierarchies felt it necessary to maintain them in a (to us) astonishing degree. He too, like Morris, looked at the facts; like Morris he did not like what he saw; yet, unlike Morris, he felt he owed it to his sense of "reality" to give those facts his limited approval.

But why should the Utopist feel that he must bow to events (facts, *res*) and their "logic" — or else bow them out? It is one thing to observe and record them and quite another to treat them with the kind of ceremonial respect which should be reserved for their motivational matrix. And that matrix is single, no matter how multiple, or contradictory, may be man's incitements to action.

II

The very term, *possibility*, has all along complicated and, in many cases, confused the Utopian mandate. Before exploring the mutual relations between what is desirable and what is possible to man, a word should be said about the conceptual range of the second term.

Possibility may be of two kinds, based either on logic or on the "facts" of the real world. Some of the greatest Utopias have been purely conceptual constructions following out, more or less strictly, certain premises laid down by the logic of the imagination. In a few cases — Leibniz' Monadology is one — the "characters" or "agents" of the piece have not even been "men" as we normally understand that term. There is no harm, and there may be a great deal of good, in purely logical Utopias so long as the writer makes his intention clear at the outset. But in many cases of this sort the intention remains ambiguous: the reader is left to speculate whether the scheme is meant to be capable of ultimate realization or whether it presents an "ideal" in the strict sense of the word (a guiding norm, *i.e.*, pattern of excellence, or else pure wish-fulfillment).

Similar difficulties arise from the use of *ultimate* in this context. These are due to the religious origin of the Utopian concern. Does *ultimate* refer to our sublunary world or is it to be read eschatologically? Again, the distinction is not always made clear by writers on the subject. In a sense, of course, all Utopias are secularized *theologoumena* (*cf.* the range and fluctuations of the word, *millennium*) but this fact does not absolve the writer from the task of definition.

The greatest confusion, then, is spread whenever both *possible* and *ultimate* remain undefined. The reader is often left unsure as to the genre of Utopia he is confronting. A strictly logical, "ideal" construction may still be viewed by its author as attainable in a life after death or even on this earth, at an imaginary "end of time." A Utopia developed in purely social terms may be so at odds with the present state of society that its realization must be placed at an incredibly distant point of human evolution. That point and the "end of time" of theology then become indistinguishable from one another for all practical purposes, and both lay reader and critic are left completely at sea. Evaluation of the total scheme and criticism of its particular features become equally impossible.

As we see it, "realizing the human potential" means no less (but also no *more*) than an optimal efficiency in the transmission and reception of electrochemical signals, transactional soundness. These transmissions and receptions are *ipso facto* "desirable," and need not be explained, much less justified, by any criterion borrowed from ethics or theology. Any organism, whether individual or social, fulfills its function in one way only: through the exercise of its biological abilities; which is to say, through profitable exchanges.

The utopian citizen will find himself confronted, as does the citizen of today, with a choice between immediate and long-range advantages; and the choice may sometimes be painful for him, as it is for us (though we assume him to be a great deal more clearheaded than ourselves when it comes to choosing, as well as virtually free of compulsions). But his choices will never be ultimate, in the sense of intending a definitive goal, or state of affairs, even as the utopian society itself lacks any feature that would give it the character of finality, permanence. Such a society knows no arbitrary limits to what may be computed as possible, on statistical grounds; yet projects that are plainly unprofitable, in terms of our earlier definition, will never reach the desk of the statistician, for the simple reason that nobody will care to *conceive* them. Projects, on the other hand, which promise substantial benefit to any or all residents of the globe will be pursued, even against heavy odds, and abandoned only if the probability of realizing them falls to zero. Neither destructive schemes nor inoffensive chimeras can survive under this dispensation: they will both wither away, not because they have been publicly outlawed or privately repressed, but through sheer inanition, lack of interest. No matter how different viciousness, destructiveness, and idle scheming or daydreaming may be from the motivational point of view, what unites them in the eyes of the operationalist is their common character of stupid wastefulness. They batten on our attention; deny them this fuel, which is so urgently needed elsewhere, and they will without fail pass out of existence.

Science cannot carry on without Utopia, nor Utopia without science. But to wed Utopia with science takes a degree of skill not available to most writers of utopian fiction, H. G. Wells and, possibly, Edward Bellamy being the only exceptions that come to mind. With Samuel Butler — certainly the most brilliant of the lot — we are already on the way (*down,* as it happens) to such negative or mock utopists as Orwell and Huxley. The reader looking for fruitful marriages between Utopia and science will have to look elsewhere: to certain treatises by Lancelot Whyte, J. B. S. Haldane, J. Arthur Thompson, all of whom were trained scientists; or to a small group of psychoanalysts — Ferenczi and Rank, chiefly — who happened to be deeply concerned with biological issues. All purely technological and economic extrapolations of our species-future have failed, and always will fail, not accidentally but necessarily; the former by focusing on sheer operation, achievement (or worse, gear and gadgets), the latter by their blind faith in the efficacy of socio-economic reform. Nor will the specialized student of history and politics — if he enlists in the Utopian cause at all, which is rare — be likely to advance it; yet the Utopist, on his side, cannot carry on his job without a profound, if somewhat paradoxical, commitment to history, which complements his equally deep commitment to science. History and science merge in the evolutionary study of human behavior: no Utopist can afford to be without a cogent behavioral model, based on the entire biological history of the species. But his locus — the place where he takes his *stand* — must inevitably be the present.

III

Each generation entertains its own image of the future, and that image is eminently historic. Even as the world has not stood still since Campanella, or Bacon, or William Morris wrote, so neither has that counterworld — no-world, no-place *(Utopos)* — stood still which forms its inevitable complement. Any yes-world requires a no-world to balance it. (The signs may be inverted; indeed, any Utopian writer will invert the conventional assignment, viewing as he must his Utopia as the world of *yes.*)

It is, then, the state of the world in which the Utopian writer finds himself that will determine his counterimage of a world-other-than-it-is. That counterimage is never the best of all possible worlds in an absolute sense: it is a world in which what is deficient in ours is supplied, except for such deficiencies as are radical, i.e., common to all man-inhabited worlds, be they actual or "merely" possible.

The first job of the Utopian writer is to take stock of the world into which he is born — to assess its total functioning. Into this assessment enters, necessarily, the entire past of the human species, but that past determines his counterworld only to the extent that it

effectively survives in present practice. Essentially, he is not interested in the past — not curious about it, as past: he is interested only
in the relation between what exists, at *his* moment in history, and
what does not now exist but might and should exist at some different
moment. (The Utopian counterworld too is seen as existing in
history, provided that term is made sufficiently comprehensive. One
of the hardest jobs confronting the Utopist is precisely this: to
extrapolate history in such a way that it *qualitatively* changes without renouncing its character as history. For man cannot escape
history, any more than he can escape himself.)

Man's conceptual apparatus being what it is, the different moment at which the Utopian counterworld is assumed to exist must
be a moment in time; and since such a world has never been known
to exist, it must be projected into the future. From this fact arise
certain embarrassments in the matter of tense; such embarrassments
cannot be wholly expunged from utopian discourse. Yet they cannot
obscure the much more fundamental fact that the Utopist speaks,
of necessity, in and from the present. Looking at the world in which
he happens to live, he finds a particular jumble of accomplishment
and failure, saturation and lack, comparable to no other such com-
pound. Perhaps the ratio of man's achievement and nonachievement
has remained roughly the same through the ages; perhaps only his
specific goals, and the motivations prompting him toward those
goals, have changed. Yet it is precisely these specific differences
in conation that concern the Utopist, for it is from them, not from
some presumed universal, that he derives his vision of possible
counterworlds. And since his stance is the present, the counterworld he himself would project must correspond — as *yes* does to
no, or *no* to *yes* — to the conative nexus our planet *presents* at
this moment.

His job then (a job performed most admirably for the end of
the Enlightenment era by William Godwin, in his *Political Justice*)
is, first, to assess as accurately as possible the assumptions under
which his own age operates, consciously, in part, but also, to no
inconsiderable degree, unconsciously — what presses it forward to
realize its ambitions in *this* particular manner and no other; and,

second, to determine both where it is failing and why. Second, his job is to propose a set of counterassumptions which would be strictly relevant to the first, in the sense that it answers them point by point, and whenever possible resolves the perplexities which have arisen from them.

It follows directly from the foregoing remarks that a contemporary Utopia cannot be plotted on elite lines: it must be capable of satisfying men or women of all sorts and conditions and the rest of the planet to boot. The classical "island" situation has become totally anachronistic, not merely because of its associations with snobbery and privilege, or its ludicrous inappropriateness in an age of jet travel and telecommunication, but because it is much too circumscribed, much too limited ecologically and otherwise, to satisfy the requirements of a genuine counterworld which could answer every complexity, every *opportunity*, of our own. The new model, then, must be large, in every sense, and, along with blessings still unknown to mankind, must include its inevitable quota of curses. All Utopists worth their salt have of course known this and tried to steer clear of the chief pitfalls of "ideal commonwealths": insipidity due to lack of normal human friction; stagnation of effort arising from "total comfort"; a beatitude made unreal by lack of contrast. Robert Frost's pungent epigram, "But Islands of the Blessèd, bless you, son;/ I never came upon a blessèd one," explodes a cozy myth but leaves the great Utopian tradition, both of the East and the West, untouched. Utopias are not, and never have been, Lotus-Isles whose inhabitants live in luxurious self-indulgence without effort and free of remorse, or Edens of innocence in which the lion and lamb lie down together. Rather, anyone who reads a body of such works cannot but be struck — even to tedium — by the pains their authors have taken to sketch the means of production and distribution, and by these same authors' resolute acceptance of forms of social injustice and malpractice — war and slavery are merely the most outstanding examples — which they number among the world's "necessary evils."

Plato, as we all know, founded his Republic on slavery. Sir Thomas More made provision for war against an aggressor and war in support of treaty obligations, and imagined much work to be done by a class of bondsmen who might be either captives or criminals. Other, later writers have chosen other dark accents for their Utopian commonwealths, not to mention those "negative utopias" in which the accents are nearly all dark. It might be said that the reading of Utopias, though a fascinating pursuit, is hardly a heartening or cheering one, inasmuch as the reader often becomes aware primarily of unfreedom, sacrifice, and effort, rather than of their opposites: freedom, increment, ease.

IV

It becomes clear that such glaring imperfections in purely imagined worlds are not merely accidental oversights, nor indices of callousness on the part of the writers who have imagined these worlds, but essential features of the Utopian enterprise, which is — as we understand it — to imagine a world order that is sensible rather than mysterious, and that has a certain relation to the world in which we live. Whether Utopia is "better" or "worse" than "real" life is not a question the asking or answering of which throws any light on the enterprise. But the question: how does it differ *is* important, as is the further question: what does this difference do to our habitual responses to the so-called "real" world? But in order to differ significantly from it, Utopia must also strikingly resemble the "real" world, and here is where the imperfections to which we alluded above have their function. Rather than slips of the pen, they are seen to be guarantees of relationship of a sort that everyone can understand. A world in which war and slavery are practiced, or a world in which a man's life is planned for him from the hour of his birth to the hour of his death, is a recognizable world in terms of our own experience of forced labor, of strife and aggression, or of a narrowly circumscribed freedom to do as we wish. By introducing these unappetizing features at the very foundation of their schemes, Utopian writers have given notice to their epochs of the seriousness with which they wished their schemes to be taken —

of the schemes' relevance, that is, to a world of strife and sorrow with which we are familiar.

It is as though the price of admission to this looking glass realm were the choosing of some familiar burden of this world, which is to be strapped on you as you travel about inside. Perhaps the penalty for losing touch with your ballast while within is never to come back at all. Certainly it is to float away into the irrelevant, the purely wishful.

As we have already stated, each individual Utopist's choice of ballast is largely determined for him — or severely narrowed, at least — by the temper of his time, i.e., his historical situation. Partly it is determined by what has or has not been done already, but even more it is guided by the complex interests of his day — the day of writing, even. For example, it seems to us that a late 20th-century Utopia is *required* to exhibit certain features which, in turn, rule out certain kinds of "ballast." We do not feel that we, personally, choose these features, but rather that we concur in them, or add our voice to the general one. For instance, such a new Utopia is required to be global in conception; to depend on technology in the widest sense; to provide grass-roots independence for all members of the society, etc. These are what we take to be broad, general aspirations of men at this time, aspirations which we share but can hardly pretend to have originated. Certain things follow from these commitments: clearly we cannot found our utopian society on slavery, as Plato did his; we are committed to the disappearance of war as both means and end; our technology has somehow to function without being "planned" from above. What, then, is to be *our* ransom, *our* guarantee that what we are doing is more serious than a pipe dream or wish for a life without annoyances and injustice? We believe that the answer to this question is to be looked for in the psychological rather than the practical field — that man is called upon to sacrifice age-old illusions and comforting fables and to see himself as much more "of a piece" than he ever has done. As a sign of this necessity, Utopian society of our day — or Utopia, 1965 — will necessarily include certain reminders of man's ancient habit of

FRANCIS & BARBARA GOLFFING : 39

fantasy-projection. Just what form these reminders take is up to each individual Utopist's imagination.

The true Utopist's pledge to reality is, at the same time, his pledge to hope: hope for a more satisfactory state of affairs than the present provides. This hope is neither a panacea nor an anodyne, though many Utopists have confused matters in the fashion of quack doctors. In strict truth, it is not even a "specific": the very idea of prescription is alien to the Utopian concern and either adulterates it or destroys it altogether. Rather than being therapeutic, Utopias are essentially diagnostic, and what they diagnose is a possible state of affairs that would be acceptable to all. This sounds like a more modest aim, but is actually the more difficult task of the two. It takes more imagination to discern the dim outlines of a workable scheme than to offer remedies for present discomforts and discontents. The office of any Utopia is to *orient* mankind: that is to say, turn men's faces toward the sun. But the only sun that matters, as every true Utopist knows, is the rising sun.

2 : Towards More Vivid Utopias

Margaret Mead

When one is asked to speak to a group primarily interested in the sciences from a platform defined by the humanities, it seems important to state more specifically where one's own discipline lies within the academic fields and what contribution one may expect to make from its specific interests. Anthropology holds a unique position, formally recognized in its inclusion in the National Research Council, where it belongs as a biological science; the Social Science Research Council, among those sciences which take man's biological nature as given; and the American Council of Learned Societies, because of its concern with language, so often defined as a pure humanity, without reference to the larynx or the delicate mechanism of the human ear.

This triple membership springs partly from the tradition of anthropological field work, in which single workers, with small funds and a narrow margin of time, visited, in what was conceived as probably the only careful study which would ever be made, small

From *Science*, vol. 126, no. 3280 (November 8, 1957), pp. 957—961.

primitive societies whose ancient and distinctive ways of life were disintegrating even as we tried to set them down. Not only did we work with urgency, as might a student of literature, trying to take down from dictation a new poem from the lips of a dying poet, or a student of painting, who found a painter of great gift drawing in an impermanent ink on the exposed, whitewashed walls of a public square — where the rain would wash it all away tomorrow or the next day — but we also, both by the nature of the situation in which we found ourselves and by the canons of our craft, looked at the whole people, at their bodies as well as at the social arrangements of their lives; at the music they made, or at least at the musical instruments with which they made it; at the dances, which might be seen as art to be appreciated as well as analyzed; at their rituals, which might be catalogued as *rites de passage* or regarded as an artistic product of generations of imaginative creativity, anonymous, time binding, with its own esthetic.

The anthropologist who works in this way comes to have an equal interest and respect for those aspects of human life which are concerned with the perception and ordering of observed regularities in nature and for those aspects of human life in which the "seeing eye" turns as much inward as outward, as the mind matches proprioception with perception in an outer world which already contains — in the shape of a roof, the line of a dance, the flick of a wrist at a sacrifice — the patterned perpetuation of earlier imaginative and creative acts.

Because we are also always committed to a scientific ordering of our material, these products of human imagination not only can be subjected to analysis of their function in a given society but can also be related to certain capacities of the human mind — themselves becoming better known through the imaginative scientific inquiries of investigators like Piaget and Inhelder, Gesell and Ilg, Erikson, and Margaret Lowenfeld. Delight in the imaginative creation of individuals or in the intuitive — that is, simultaneous and so unanalyzed — grasp of these as wholes by whole societies, does not prevent analytic work, also. The two methods of approach — that of the humanities, which focuses upon a recognition of the unique character of a work of the imagination, and that of the sciences, which attempts by careful observation, analysis, and finally experiment to understand the lawfulness of the behavior involved — can be used.

VISION AND CULTURES

It is from this particular background of research that I wish to describe the role which men's visions of a possible and more desirable future play in the development of a culture. Utopias may be seen from many points of view — as projections from individual experience; as projections from individual experiences stamped by the point of view of a particular period; as sterile blueprints, too narrow to confine the natural varieties of the human mind for very long, as when they are lived out by small cult groups who pare and mold the individuals born within them to a confining and crippling mode. Or they may be seen as those visions of future possibilities which lead the minds of men forward into the future, giving life a meaning beyond the grave or beyond the simple domestic perpetuation of one's own life in the lives of one's children, with an interest in the trees planted in one's own garden but no interest in the trees in one's neighbors' gardens. The Golden Age, a retrospective utopia of the days when all men lived like gods, and walked and talked with gods — the days before death or work or separation came into the world — may also, of course, play a significant role in keeping a whole people caught in a dream unrelated to the requirements of the contemporary world.

Using models from primitive cultures, we may, from this point of view, look at those cultures in which life is held steady by a view of the past, of which the present is a poor copy, a vale of tears where once there was Olympian laughter, at those cultures which live a hand-to-mouth existence, wrapped in the small urgencies of the present, and at those which move, generation after generation, toward Heaven — which may be the heavenly Jerusalem "with milk and honey blest," the Jerusalem to be rebuilt and reinhabited, which informed the imagination of Jews throughout the Diaspora, or the Jerusalem to be built "in England's green and pleasant land." Against these may be placed Nirvana, with its insistent comment on the lack of value in all earthly and individualized life.

Within a culture as complex as our own, which draws on the inheritance of so many earlier and partly recorded pasts and which now has available an even larger number of incomparable and imaginatively stimulating "presents," from accounts of the peoples whose lives were part of a different stream — in Africa, in the Orient, and in the New World — it is obvious that we may live not only on different visions at different periods but also on different and incompatible visions at the same time. Part of the excitement and the difficulty of the modern world, which makes the artist feel that he has no whole context within which to create his personal, special new vision and which makes the scientist turn to the anonymous writing of science fiction nightmares, is just the way in which different sorts of utopias — one man's dream and another man's nightmare — jostle each other even within the confines of one political speech or one brief editorial, as we yearn for a past, rage at or delight in the present, or promise or threaten a future. While it always has been and will probably always be the mark of the more educated man that he lives in a longer time perspective, both into the past and into the future, than his less well educated contemporaries, where this education is underwritten by no habitual pattern of thought and speech within which such time perspectives are implicitly expressed, the presence of so many and such contrasting world views may seem fragmenting and mechanical rather than living.

OF PRACTICAL IMPORT

Yet, from comparative materials, it seems quite clear that the utopias men live by are of vital importance in such mundane matters as whether they will struggle to preserve the identity of their society, their class, their religion, or their vocation; whether they will plant trees which take two lifetimes to mature; whether they will take thought to stop the forests from being depleted, the good soil from being washed into the sea, or the gene pool from becoming exposed to too much radiation. Men who believe that the ultimate good state will mean the abolition of identity are hardly likely to take an active interest in public health, and those who believe that the Day of Judgment is near, when the sheep will be separated from the goats and the whole world will go up in a holocaust directed by a punishing Deity, see the atom bomb as an addition to the Lord's armory of destruction.

Within any determinedly other-worldly religion, there is a perpetual conflict between the active acceptance of early death (so the little, innocent souls may go up to God at once, unstained by sin) and the need for public health measures and preventive medicine as well as for the compassionate dole to the beggar or care for the dying. The Catholic Church has fought a long battle against an otherworldliness which would have as its logic an overvaluation of death — which has occasionally been the response of literal-minded savages to enthusiastic Christian preaching about heaven. On the other hand, the modern public health movement has its problems in an overvaluation of the importance of individual life, which leads to a lowering of death rates before there is a compensating rise in the standard of living and a fall in the birth rate, with the result that famine and misery are the portion of the very individuals whose lives were to be bettered.

THE PALLID UTOPIAS

At the same time, all visions of heaven, in this world and in the next, have a curiously tasteless, pale blue and pink quality, whether the image is one of cherubim and seraphim "casting down their golden crowns around the glassy sea" or of a time when "ploughs in peaceful industry shall supersede the sword," when "the dictatorship of the proletariat shall be realized in ideological completeness," or when lions shall lie down with lambs, or of a world in which women shall have been freed from all the incidental consequences of their reproductivity and will spend long vacations with their lovers of the moment, flying Chinese kites.

Beside any picture of heaven above or heaven on earth, the pictures of hell and destruction stand out in vivid and compelling intensity, each detail strong enough to grip the imagination as the horrid creations of a Wells, an Orwell, or an Aldous Huxley unroll before our horrified eyes. Where positive utopias are insipid and a detailed heaven is unbearable to think of as a permanent abode, the creators of terror, the repudiators of man's future, have no such problem. So, if utopian visions are the stuff by which men live, it would seem a legitimate subject of inquiry to ask what is the matter with them? Why is Hell always so much more vivid than Heaven? Why, as I heard a young priest say recently, are all images of heaven "while not exactly not true, not as true as they might be"?

There have been attempts to give scientific answers to this question: that the prefiguration of bliss lies in the womb, where the child has no chance to use its distance receptors, and so the feeling remains one of undifferentiated and unspecified ecstasy; that analysis destroys a vision by introducing an element of self-consciousness and detachment of part of the self. These may be adequate explanations of the way in which the individual, in terms of his life experience, seeks for or experiences visionary ecstasy, but they seem insufficient answers to the problem of why the imagination of the human race, which has produced its long procession of great creations, has never yet succeeded in building a picture of a future really unlike the present, either in this world or in the next, where anyone passionately wished to live except when it was counterpointed against a Hell, delineated with the greatest precision. Heaven and all the pallid utopias are, in fact, even like Nirvana, blank white spaces — or spaces a little tinted with pastel and furnished with plastic gadgets — and are given reality only by contrast with the fear, pain, and agony of some other state.

Yet it is by visions of a better world or place or state that men make positive efforts — in contrast to fiddling while Rome burns or refraining from evil all their days in fear of hell-fire. So it would seem legitimate to ask why human imaginations are, apparently, so handicapped in the creation of such essential visions and whether there is any way in which our present scientific knowledge of human behavior and of the way in which societies function can be used to create conditions within which utopias might be created whose positive hold on men's minds would be stronger than the negative hold of the Infernos and Lost Paradises. For the last 50 years we have experimented with the compelling character of negative images, as the prophecies of the dangers of modern warfare have grown ever sharper. When warfare is upon them, men will struggle; but they sink into a kind of paralysis when there is need to fight even harder —in peacetime — to prevent a recurrence of war. We need more vivid utopias.

One answer to the question comes from an examination of the struggle that institutionalized religions, which present the other world as desirable, must go through to deal with suicide, either condemning it as a dereliction in stewardship, as Christianity does, and treating the living out of life on earth as a trust, or hedging it around with terribly difficult steps, as in parts of India, where, in order to die a holy and self-elected death, a man must give up caste and family and must become purified until, at last, dressed for the next world and in a trance, he is lowered into the earth "alive." The next world must not be so desirable that it completely competes with this one and leads a majority of believers to suicide or toward a too-willing death in war, with the promise of a warriors' heaven. A long life of preparation — as a shaven and dedicated celibate, completely cloistered or moving through the streets with a begging bowl and making a contribution to the ongoing life of the world as teacher, nurse, or supplicant — this is feasible.

Similarly, Communism has always had difficulties with those who, regarding the Soviet Union as heaven on earth, have wished to go and live there instead of remaining in their own unregenerate countries, working at dull organizational jobs in the hope of a World Revolution which they themselves might not live to see. Sometimes short trips to the Soviet Union, as circumscribed as visions of the next world to a cloistered religious, were permitted. But the tension between the vision and the present must not include any way of immediately slackening it by a self-elected entry into heaven.

DREAMS—COMPELLING AND TEMPERED

In fact, through the emphasis on dedication, attention is shifted from the self to the fate of others; through prayer for the souls in purgatory, teaching the young, or preparing for the revolution from which others will benefit, the necessary distance seems to be created so that a vision can be compelling, drawing one on like a magnet, but not too fast or too far. So perhaps it may be said that it is only when the visionary or the prophet, the poet or the painter wants to involve the individual directly in the future vision that the danger of immediate response is allowed for in the interpreters and spectators by a dilution of its intensity. Then Heaven or the Perfect Socialist State may be seen as being too insipid and as tasting like sawdust. A feeling of less involvement may be achieved by concentrating the individual's effort on the relation between someone else and the desired state — where the nexus can have both the intensity of devotion to the other and devotion to the dream without the temptation to relax and try to get there oneself.

Even here the other temptation — to force history at once to disgorge a visionary paradise at no matter what cost of suffering and death — is present as soon as Heaven is too vividly conceived even for the other, who must then be saved, by the rack or by brain washing, to become a denizen of someone else's too compelling dream. The ability of any people to cultivate protective devices against other people's compelling visions — against which the best defenses seem to be either laughter or else revolt against any individual being in thrall to the will of another — must also be considered as one component in their ability to create utopian dreams which inspire but do not limit them.

APPEAL TO UNIVERSALS

But there seems also to be another explanation of the relative lack of vividness of the good vision as compared with the nightmare. In pictures of Hell, of dictatorships armed with concentration camps and thought control, the appeal is made to human beings' most shared and least differentiated responses; pain, hunger, thirst, being bound, tortured, cut off from other human beings, and battered day and night by intolerable stimuli — these are experiences which repel every human being and under which the savage and the civilized, the illiterate and the scholar, ultimately break down.

Men of different temperaments will break in different ways and at different points, but the effect of Medieval images of the tortures of Hell, when conjured up by a gifted preacher, or of the tortures actually administered in Nazi and Communist prisons is, in the end, to break all but the exceptional martyr sustained by a vision (which, only in this exceptional situation, cannot be called too vivid) of another world to which he is personally totally committed. (So Jehovah's Witnesses are said to stand up well to Communist pressures, and Orthodox Jews went chanting to the gas chambers as the early Christians, in the days when the Second Coming was felt to be very near, faced the lions.)

APPEAL TO DIVERSITY

But the utopian vision, which is vivid enough to compel men's imagination and yet not so compelling that men must resort to rack and torture to bring others into it — the vision which men want to share with others and entrust to their expanding imagination rather than the vision in which they wish to entrap and imprison others — is built not upon the universals of fear and pain, hunger and thirst, ultimate fatigue and weakness, but upon the great diversity of human propensities and gifts. It must be, in terms of modern information theory, redundant enough to catch the developed imagination of each so-different member of any society.

Reduction to fear and pain gives men a common basis of the unbearable which can be elaborated — a nightmare peopled with Sisyphus endlessly rolling his stone and Tityus in agony. But reduction to our common good human experience leaves us with images of milk and honey, which stand very little elaboration before they are disintegrated by the involvement of our specific imaginations, by the differences in our childhood images of love and trust and bliss: it was not honey but strawberry jam, not the hum of bees but the flash of dragonfly wings, not a pointed breast but a round one which gave one suck. The recitation of such particular delights of food and drink as goat's milk or palm wine, durian, or witchetty grubs only resonate in the minds of those who once drank or ate them and fall dead upon the ears of those who never knew these pleasures. A whole society can be drawn on only by a utopian vision which contains the separate experiences of different regions, different classes, and different vocations, combined with the varied notes on each theme played by men of different temperament, disciplined and shaped by the prevailing forms of the culture. So it is no wonder that utopias are hard to come by.

THE WORLD'S NEEDS

Yet the world today is sorely in need of a vision which will endow our lives with meaning and responsibility and will make safe the terrible powers of destruction and the almost limitless powers of construction which scientific research has put into our hands. We can specify some of the characteristics this vision must have: it must be vivid enough to compel the heart, but not so vivid that one moves too quickly, by death or emigration or the coercion of others, to attain it; it must be so conceived that it is sought for the sake of others rather than solely for the self — for other men, for the whole next generation, or for men eons ahead — with nice adjustments which make it not too immediate (just the next generation) and not too distant, lest one become lost in a world without imaginable relation to the present; and it must be complex, redundant enough to catch and hold the imaginations of men and women of many different types of temperament and experience, and stylized enough, in terms of culture and period, to carry the weight of past ages of formal esthetic molding and polishing and to speak with cadences and lines grown powerful by long usage.

These prescriptions I am giving are of the sort which can be derived from the scientific comparison of cultures; they are prescriptions for conditions. So one may compare ages and countries in which a particular art or science has flourished with those in which they have not so flourished, dissect out what appear to be the facilitating conditions, list and describe them.

Possibly all these may be necessary but not sufficient causes. Yet it is by the specification and attempted realization of conditions within which events desired and deemed necessary may occur that the sciences that deal with man can work in the world, stating conditions within which a child can grow, an idea can take root, an institution can flourish, and a man's hand and eye can grow cunning, his mind sharp, and his imagination wide. Though we remain dependent upon the caliber of individuals for our great achievements, the contrasts between one culture and another — between peoples whose every movement is a work of art and peoples, of the same human species, who limit their artistry to a few scratches on the edge of a pot — leave little doubt that the cultural conditions for any kind of creativity are very important. And as, by the scientific comparative study of cultures, we learn more about them, we can turn from hand-wringing, viewing with alarm, and the role of Cassandra to build the world closer to our heart's desire.

NECESSARY CONDITIONS

What, then, may the conditions be within which we may foster more vivid utopias? Three resources which seem accessible to us with our present knowledge are these: the imaginations of little children, where each newborn child brings a unique and new potential to our perception and ordering of the world; the provision of materials from other cultures, so that in the interplay between the great achievements of the human race in the many separate, unique, but comparable cultures men have built, new combinations and forms may occur; and the creation of conditions within which those who know the possibilities for the future, which are emerging from scientific discoveries, can combine their insights with the insights of those who know the full and astounding range of what man has achieved in the past, without mutations or the hypertrophies of extrasensory perception currently invoked by the creators of our folklore of the future, the writers of science fiction.

THE CHILD'S PERCEPTION

The imaginative capacities of young children, initially part of the processes of growth and evolution, as Edith Cobb has phrased it, are then one source to which we must turn. Within the growing child, the capacity to bring order out of the perception of the outside world and the capacity to create something unique and new out of his perception of himself in the world are, initially, two parts of one process. Concentration on one at the expense of the other robs the child, and so the world, of what could have come from both.

The current experiments of Jean Piaget and Barbel Inhelder in Geneva provide a vivid illustration of these two approaches. Piaget and Inhelder have developed a set of experiments to test the child's growing capacity to recognize some of the principles essential to scientfic thought. One of these, which Piaget calls "reversibility," is exemplified in the child's recognition that when a large round lump of clay is thinned out to a narrow cylinder, it will still have the same weight and be the same amount of clay. When these experiments are reported only in words, with the emphasis placed upon growth, with chronological age and school training, of the ability to recognize such points, the *other* things the child does are catalogued simply as failure. But when a method of reporting is used which records the entire behavior of children at different ages — through sound film, film and tape, or the verbatim recording of words — then the whole child comes into the picture and we see something else.

Thus, in the test situation the child is presented with a laboratory apparatus by which a colored fluid can be released gradually from the upper glass chamber, through a cock, into a glass below. The child is shown how this works and is allowed to try it. Then he is given series of cards picturing the state of the apparatus before any fluid enters the glass, at various stages, and finally, when all of it has entered the glass. The card series are presented to the child in a scrambled state, and the child is asked to arrange them. One little boy, whose achievement on the test — like that of many children of his age — would have been reported as "failure," made a response which can be described as poetic as he "rhymed" the cards instead of arranging them to represent the reality of colored water passing into a glass in an orderly way. Using the same materials, he drew on another capacity of his mind. Had this been a class in "design" or in "making pleasing patterns," his answer would have been the "right" answer, whereas when he was being tested for ability to use a kind of thinking basic to modern science, it was a "wrong" answer.

In the kind of training given in European schools of the Swiss type, the child has to learn to handle this kind of reversibility after first encountering a world in which rigid one-way sequences in behavior and among material things have been heavily emphasized. By contrast, it is the problem of how to handle rigid sequences — which cannot be reversed in fact, however they may be reversed in thought — that must be learned by the first generation of a people who encounter factory methods, people who have arranged life in their heads in poetic patterns and who have not been told that this is the "wrong" answer. Recently I saw a group of educated men and women who had been presented with some similar problems in building manifolds by means of brightly colored units; the men classified the exercise as "art" and, although they were much better in mathematics and science in college than the women, failed, while the women, who also classified the exercise as "art," at which they thought themselves good, succeeded easily. By failing to cultivate both sides of the child's ability, by opposing them and negating one or the other, we are losing not only artists but also scientists, and we

are splitting our society, as well as our individual children, into incompatible parts, destructively at war with each other. A different
type of education, which recognizes the early stage in which children
can apprehend form through color and kinesthetic feel and the recognition of sets, is a precondition for preserving the creativity with
which each generation of newborn children enters the world.

A WHOLE VIEW OF THE PAST

The second necessary condition, a knowledge of what men have
done before, again involves the presentation of wholes — not the
current split between the history of science and technology, on the
one hand, and art museums and literature courses, on the other. In
real life the imagination of the painter and the poet are essential to
the conditions within which the scientist works, for the fearful
presage of the poet reaches ahead of invention. A few years ago an
attempt was made to design an exhibition which would show the
effect upon painting of modern scientific invention in building design; but in looking at the materials it was discovered that in every
case the painter's vision had preceded the necessary technological
invention, as the myth of Icarus preceded the Wright brothers. So
we need arrangements which will bring together, for the experience
of the student and the adult, whole historic periods — their buildings and their ideas, their books and their economics, their painting
and their technology, their mathematics and their poetry — so that
out of the perceived relationships and comparisons among them new
ideas may be born and the present ignorance among scientists of
man's past and present greatness, surpassed only by the ignorance
among most humanists and many artists of man's future, made possible by science, may be overcome.

"CHAIRS OF THE FUTURE"

Finally, it seems to me, in this age when the very survival of the
human race and possibly of all living creatures depends upon our
having a vision of the future for others which will command our

deepest commitment, we need in our universities, which must change and grow with the world, not only chairs of history and comparative linguistics, of literature and art — which deal with the past and sometimes with the present — but we need also Chairs of the Future, chairs for those who will devote themselves, with all the necessary scholarship and attention, to developing science to the full extent of its possibilities for the future, and who will devote themselves as faithfully to the fine detail of what man might very well — in the light of all our knowledge — be as any classicist or medievalist devotes himself to the texts of Pindar and Horace or to the thought of St. Thomas Aquinas.

BIBLIOGRAPHY

M. Carstairs, *The Twice Born* (Hogarth, London), in press.

E. Cobb, "The ecology of imagination in childhood," unpublished.

E. H. Erikson, *Childhood and Society* (Norton, New York, 1950).

L. K. Frank, "Imagination in education," in *Imagination in Education,* Proceedings of the Bank Street College Conference (Bank Street College of Education, New York, 1956), pp. 64-72.

A. Gesell and F. Ilg, *Infant and Child in the Culture of Today* (Harper, New York, 1946).

W. Grey-Walter, *The Curve of the Snowflake* (Norton, New York, 1956).

G. R. Harrison, *What Man May Be, The Human Side of Science* (Morrow, New York, 1956).

G. Hendrix, "Prerequisites to meaning," *Math. Teacher,* 43, 334 (1950).

M. Lowenfeld, "The world pictures of children, a method of recording and studying them," *Brit. J. Med. Psychol.,* 18, pt. 1, 65 (1939); "Poleidoblocs" (forthcoming series of tests on children's mathematical imagination; available at the Institute for Child Psychology, London).

M. Mead, "Arts in Bali," *Yale Rev.,* 30, 335 (1940); "On the implications for anthropology of the Gesell-Ilg approach to maturation," *Am. Anthropologist,* 49, 69 (1947); "Some relationships between social anthropology and psychiatry," in *Dynamic Psychiatry,* F. Alexander and H. Ross, Eds. (Univ. of Chicago Press, Chicago, 1952), pp. 401-448; "Cultural discontinuities and personality transformation," *J. Social Issues* (Kurt Lewin Memorial Award Issue, Suppl. Ser., No. 8).

C. Morris, *Varieties of Human Values* (Univ. of Chicago Press, Chicago, 1956).

J. Piaget, *Le développement de la notion de temps chez l'enfant* (Presses Universitaires de France, Paris, 1946), chap. 1, pp. 5-36.

E. Sewell, *The Field of Nonsense* (Chatto and Windus, London, 1952).

J. Tanner and B. Inhelder, Eds., *Psycho-biological Development of the Child* (International Universities Press, New York, 1956; 1957), vols. 1, 2.

3: Freedom and the Control of Men

B. F. Skinner

The second half of the twentieth century may be remembered for its solution of a curious problem. Although Western democracy created the conditions responsible for the rise of modern science, it is now evident that it may never fully profit from that achievement. The so-called "democratic philosophy" of human behavior to which it also gave rise is increasingly in conflict with the application of the methods of science to human affairs. Unless this conflict is somehow resolved, the ultimate goals of democracy may be long deferred.

I

Just as biographers and critics look for external influences to account for the traits and achievements of the men they study, so science ultimately explains behavior in terms of "causes" or condi-

From *The American Scholar,* vol. 25, no. 1 (Winter 1955-1956), pp. 47-65. Reprinted in B. F. Skinner, *Cumulative Record* (New York: Appleton, rev. ed. 1961).

tions which lie beyond the individual himself. As more and more causal relations are demonstrated, a practical corollary becomes difficult to resist: it should be possible to *produce* behavior according to plan simply by arranging the proper conditions. Now, among the specifications which might reasonably be submitted to a behavioral technology are these: Let men be happy, informed, skillful, well behaved, and productive.

This immediate practical implication of a science of behavior has a familiar ring, for it recalls the doctrine of human perfectibility of eighteenth- and nineteenth-century humanism. A science of man shares the optimism of that philosophy and supplies striking support for the working faith that men can build a better world and, through it, better men. The support comes just in time, for there has been little optimism of late among those who speak from the traditional point of view. Democracy has become "realistic," and it is only with some embarrassment that one admits today to perfectionistic or utopian thinking.

The earlier temper is worth considering, however. History records many foolish and unworkable schemes for human betterment, but almost all the great changes in our culture which we now regard as worthwhile can be traced to perfectionistic philosophies. Governmental, religious, educational, economic, and social reforms follow a common pattern. Someone believes that a change in a cultural practice — for example, in the rules of evidence in a court of law, in the characterization of man's relation to God, in the way children are taught to read and write, in permitted rates of interest, or in minimal housing standards — will improve the condition of men: by promoting justice, permitting men to seek salvation more effectively, increasing the literacy of a people, checking an inflationary trend, or improving public health and family relations, respectively. The underlying hypothesis is always the same: that a different physical or cultural environment will make a different and better man.

The scientific study of behavior not only justifies the general pattern of such proposals; it promises new and better hypotheses. The earliest cultural practices must have originated in sheer accidents. Those which strengthened the group survived with the group in a sort of natural selection. As soon as men began to propose and carry out changes in practice for the sake of possible consequences, the evolutionary process must have accelerated. The simple practice of making changes must have had survival value. A further acceleration is now to be expected. As laws of behavior are more precisely stated, the changes in the environment required to bring about a given effect may be more clearly specified. Conditions which have been neglected because their effects were slight or unlooked for may be shown to be relevant. New conditions may actually be created, as in the discovery and synthesis of drugs which affect behavior.

This is no time, then, to abandon notions of progress, improvement or, indeed, human perfectibility. The simple fact is that man is able, and now as never before, to lift himself by his own bootstraps. In achieving control of the world of which he is a part, he may learn at last to control himself.

II

Timeworn objections to the planned improvement of cultural practices are already losing much of their force. Marcus Aurelius was probably right in advising his readers to be content with a haphazard amelioration of mankind. "Never hope to realize Plato's republic," he sighed, "...for who can change the opinions of men? And without a change of sentiments what can you make but reluctant slaves and hypocrites?" He was thinking, no doubt, of contemporary patterns of control based upon punishment or the threat of punishment which, as he correctly observed, breed only reluctant slaves of those who submit and hypocrites of those who discover modes of evasion. But we need not share his pessimism, for the opinions of men can be changed. The techniques of indoctrination which were being devised by the early Christian Church at the very time Marcus Aurelius was writing are relevant, as are some of the techniques of psychotherapy and of advertising and public relations. Other methods suggested by recent scientific analyses leave little doubt of the matter.

The study of human behavior also answers the cynical complaint that there is a plain "cussedness" in man which will always thwart efforts to improve him. We are often told that men do not want to be changed, even for the better. Try to help them, and they will outwit you and remain happily wretched. Dostoevsky claimed to see some plan in it. "Out of sheer ingratitude," he complained, or possibly boasted, "man will play you a dirty trick, just to prove that men are still men and not the keys of a piano.... And even if you could prove that a man is only a piano key, he would still do something out of sheer perversity — he would create destruction and chaos — just to gain his point.... And if all this could in turn be analyzed and prevented by predicting that it would occur, then man would deliberately go mad to prove his point." This is a conceivable neurotic reaction to inept control. A few men may have shown it, and many have enjoyed Dostoevsky's statement because they tend to show it. But that such perversity is a fundamental reaction of the human organism to controlling conditions is sheer nonsense.

So is the objection that we have no way of knowing what changes to make even though we have the necessary techniques. That is one of the great hoaxes of the century — a sort of booby trap left behind in the retreat before the advancing front of science. Scientists themselves have unsuspectingly agreed that there are two kinds of useful propositions about nature — facts and value judgments — and that science must confine itself to "what is," leaving "what ought to be" to others. But with what special sort of wisdom is the nonscientist endowed? Science is only effective knowing, no matter who engages in it. Verbal behavior proves upon analysis to be composed of many different types of utterances, from poetry and exhortation to logic and factual description, but these are not all equally useful in talking about cultural practices. We may classify useful propositions according to the degrees of confidence with which they may be asserted. Sentences about nature range from highly probable "facts" to sheer guesses. In general, future events are less likely to be correctly described than past. When a scientist talks about a projected experiment, for example, he often resorts to statements having a moderate likelihood of being correct; he calls them hypotheses.

Designing a new cultural pattern is in many ways like designing an experiment. In drawing up a new constitution, outlining a new educational program, modifying a religious doctrine, or setting up a new fiscal policy, many statements must be quite tentative. We cannot be sure that the practices we specify will have the consequences we predict, or that the consequences will reward our efforts. This is in the nature of such proposals. They are not value judgments — they are guesses. To confuse and delay the improvement of cultural practices by quibbling about the word *improve* is itself not a useful practice. Let us agree, to start with, that health is better than illness, wisdom better than ignorance, love better than hate, and productive energy better than neurotic sloth.

Another familiar objection is the "political problem." Though we know what changes to make and how to make them, we still need to control certain relevant conditions, but these have long since fallen into the hands of selfish men who are not going to relinquish them for such purposes. Possibly we shall be permitted to develop areas which at the moment seem unimportant, but at the first signs of success the strong men will move in. This, it is said, has happened to Christianity, democracy, and communism. There will always be men who are fundamentally selfish and evil, and in the long run innocent goodness cannot have its way. The only evidence here is historical, and it may be misleading. Because of the way in which physical science developed, history could until very recently have "proved" that the unleashing of the energy of the atom was quite unlikely, if not impossible. Similarly, because of the order in which processes in human behavior have become available for purposes of control, history may seem to prove that power will probably be appropriated for selfish purposes. The first techniques to be discovered fell almost always to strong, selfish men. History led Lord Acton to believe that power corrupts, but he had probably never encountered absolute power, certainly not in all its forms, and had no way of predicting its effect.

An optimistic historian could defend a different conclusion. The principle that if there are not enough men of good will in the world the first step is to create more seems to be gaining recognition. The

Marshall Plan (as originally conceived), Point Four, the offer of atomic materials to power-starved countries — these may or may not be wholly new in the history of international relations, but they suggest an increasing awareness of the power of governmental good will. They are proposals to make certain changes in the environments of men for the sake of consequences which should be rewarding for all concerned. They do not exemplify a disinterested generosity, but an interest which is the interest of everyone. We have not yet seen Plato's philosopher-king, and may not want to, but the gap between real and utopian government is closing.

III

But we are not yet in the clear, for a new and unexpected obstacle has arisen. With a world of their own making almost within reach, men of good will have been seized with distaste for their achievement. They have uneasily rejected opportunities to apply the techniques and findings of science in the service of men, and as the import of effective cultural design has come to be understood, many of them have voiced an outright refusal to have any part in it. Science has been challenged before when it has encroached upon institutions already engaged in the control of human behavior; but what are we to make of benevolent men, with no special interests of their own to defend, who nevertheless turn against the very means of reaching long-dreamed-of goals?

What is being rejected, of course, is the scientific conception of man and his place in nature. So long as the findings and methods of science are applied to human affairs only in a sort of remedial patchwork, we may continue to hold any view of human nature we like. But as the use of science increases, we are forced to accept the theoretical structure with which science represents its facts. The difficulty is that this structure is clearly at odds with the traditional democratic conception of man. Every discovery of an event which has a part in shaping a man's behavior seems to leave so much the less to be credited to the man himself; and as such explanations become more and more comprehensive, the contribution which may be claimed by the individual himself appears to approach zero. Man's vaunted creative powers, his original accomplishments in art, science, and morals, his capacity to choose and our right to hold him responsible for the consequences of his choice — none of these is conspicuous in this new self-portrait. Man, we once believed, was free to express himself in art, music, and literature, to inquire into nature, to seek salvation in his own way. He could initiate action and make spontaneous and capricious changes of course. Under the most extreme duress some sort of choice remained to him. He could resist any effort to control him, though it might cost him his life. But science insists that action is initiated by forces impinging upon the individual, and that caprice is only another name for behavior for which we have not yet found a cause.

In attempting to reconcile these views it is important to note that the traditional democratic conception was not designed as a description in the scientific sense but a philosophy to be used in setting up and maintaining a governmental process. It arose under historical circumstances and served political purposes apart from which it cannot be properly understood. In rallying men against tyranny it was necessary that the individual be strengthened, that he be taught that he had rights and could govern himself. To give the common man a new conception of his worth, his dignity, and his power to save himself, both here and hereafter, was often the only resource of the revolutionist. When democratic principles were put into practice, the same doctrines were used as a working formula. This is exemplified by the notion of personal responsibility in Anglo-American law. All governments make certain forms of punishment contingent upon certain kinds of acts. In democratic countries these contingencies are expressed by the notion of responsible choice. But the notion may have no meaning under governmental practices formulated in other ways and would certainly have no place in systems which did not use punishment.

The democratic philosophy of human nature is determined by certain political exigencies and techniques, not by the goals of democracy. But exigencies and techniques change; and a conception which is not supported for its accuracy as a likeness — is not, indeed, rooted in fact at all — may be expected to change too. No matter how effective we judge current democratic practices to be, how highly we value them or how long we expect them to survive, they are almost certainly not the *final* form of government. The philosophy of human nature which has been useful in implementing them is also almost certainly not the last word. The ultimate achievement of democracy may be long deferred unless we emphasize the real aims rather than the verbal devices of democratic thinking. A philosophy which has been appropriate to one set of political exigencies will defeat its purpose if, under other circumstances, it prevents us from applying to human affairs the science of man which probably nothing but democracy itself could have produced.

IV

Perhaps the most crucial part of our democratic philosophy to be reconsidered is our attitude toward freedom — or its reciprocal, the control of human behavior. We do not oppose all forms of control because it is "human nature" to do so. The reaction is not characteristic of all men under all conditions of life. It is an attitude which has been carefully engineered, in large part by what we call the "literature" of democracy. With respect to some methods of control (for example, the threat of force), very little engineering is needed, for the techniques or their immediate consequences are objectionable. Society has suppressed these methods by branding them "wrong," "illegal," or "sinful." But to encourage these attitudes toward objectionable forms of control, it has been necessary to disguise the real nature of certain indispensable techniques, the commonest examples of which are education, persuasion, and moral discourse. The actual procedures appear harmless enough. They consist of supplying information, presenting opportunities for action, pointing out logical relationships, appealing to reason or "enlightened understanding," and so on. Through a masterful piece of misrepresentation, the illusion is fostered that these procedures do not involve the control of behavior; at most, they are simply ways of "getting someone to change his mind." But analysis not only reveals the presence of well-defined behavioral processes, it demonstrates a kind of control no less inexorable, though in some ways more acceptable, than the bully's threat of force.

Let us suppose that someone in whom we are interested is acting unwisely — he is careless in the way he deals with his friends, he drives too fast, or he holds his golf club the wrong way. We could probably help him by issuing a series of commands: don't nag, don't drive over sixty, don't hold your club that way. Much less objectionable would be "an appeal to reason." We could show him how people are affected by his treatment of them, how accident rates rise sharply at higher speeds, how a particular grip on the club alters the way the ball is struck and corrects a slice. In doing so we resort to verbal mediating devices which emphasize and support certain "contingencies of reinforcement" — that is, certain relations between behavior and its consequences — which strengthen the behavior we wish to set up. The same consequences would possibly set up the behavior without our help, and they eventually take control no matter which form of help we give. The appeal to reason has certain advantages over the authoritative command. A threat of punishment, no matter how subtle, generates emotional reactions and tendencies to escape or revolt. Perhaps the controllee merely "feels resentment" at being made to act in a given way, but even that is to be avoided. When we "appeal to reason," he "feels freer to do as he pleases." The fact is that we have exerted *less* control than in using a threat; since other conditions may contribute to the result, the effect may be delayed or, possibly in a given instance, lacking. But if we have worked a change in his behavior at all, it is because we have altered relevant environmental conditions, and the processes we have set in motion are just as real and just as inexorable, if not as comprehensive, as in the most authoritative coercion.

"Arranging an opportunity for action" is another example of disguised control. The power of the negative form has already been exposed in the analysis of censorship. Restriction of opportunity is recognized as far from harmless. As Ralph Barton Perry said in an article which appeared in the Spring 1953 *Pacific Spectator,* "Whoever determines what alternatives shall be made known to man controls what that man shall choose *from*. He is deprived of freedom in proportion as he is denied access to *any* ideas, or is confined to any range of ideas short of the totality of relevant possibilities." But there is a positive side as well. When we present a relevant state of affairs, we increase the likelihood that a given form of behavior will be emitted. To the extent that the probability of action has changed, we have made a definite contribution. The teacher of history controls a student's behavior (or, if the reader prefers, "deprives him of freedom") just as much in *presenting* historical facts as in suppressing them. Other conditions will no doubt affect the student, but the contribution made to his behavior by the presentation of material is fixed and, within its range, irresistible.

The methods of education, moral discourse, and persuasion are acceptable not because they recognize the freedom of the individual or his right to dissent, but because they make only *partial* contributions to the control of his behavior. The freedom they recognize is freedom from a more coercive form of control. The dissent which they tolerate is the possible effect of other determiners of action. Since these sanctioned methods are frequently ineffective, we have been able to convince ourselves that they do not represent control at all. When they show too much strength to permit disguise, we give them other names and suppress them as energetically as we suppress the use of force. Education grown too powerful is rejected as propaganda or "brain-washing," while really effective persuasion is decried as "undue influence," "demagoguery," "seduction," and so on.

If we are not to rely solely upon accident for the innovations which give rise to cultural evolution, we must accept the fact that some kind of control of human behavior is inevitable. We cannot use good sense in human affairs unless someone engages in the design and construction of environmental conditions which affect the behavior of men. Environmental changes have always been the condition for the improvement of cultural patterns, and we can hardly use the more effective methods of science without making changes on a grander scale. We are all controlled by the world in which we live, and part of that world has been and will be constructed by men. The question is this: Are we to be controlled by accident, by tyrants, or by ourselves in effective cultural design?

The danger of the misuse of power is possibly greater than ever. It is not allayed by disguising the facts. We cannot make wise decisions if we continue to pretend that human behavior is not controlled, or if we refuse to engage in control when valuable results might be forthcoming. Such measures weaken only ourselves, leaving the strength of science to others. The first step in a defense against tyranny is the fullest possible exposure of controlling techniques. A second step has already been taken successfully in restricting the use of physical force. Slowly, and as yet imperfectly, we have worked out an ethical and governmental design in which the strong man is not allowed to use the power deriving from his strength to control his fellow men. He is restrained by a superior force created for that purpose — the ethical pressure of the group, or more explicit religious and governmental measures. We tend to distrust superior forces, as we currently hesitate to relinquish sovereignty in order to set up an international police force. But it is only through such countercontrol that we have achieved what we call peace — a condition in which men are not permitted to control each other through force. In other words, control itself must be controlled.

Science has turned up dangerous processes and materials before. To use the facts and techniques of a science of man to the fullest extent without making some monstrous mistake will be difficult and obviously perilous. It is no time for self-deception, emotional indulgence, or the assumption of attitudes which are no longer useful. Man is facing a difficult test. He must keep his head now, or he must start again — a long way back.

V

Those who reject the scientific conception of man must, to be logical, oppose the methods of science as well. The position is often supported by predicting a series of dire consequences which are to follow if science is not checked. A recent book by Joseph Wood Krutch, *The Measure of Man,* is in this vein. Mr. Krutch sees in the growing science of man the threat of an unexampled tyranny over men's minds. If science is permitted to have its way, he insists, "we may never be able really to think again." A controlled culture will, for example, lack some virtue inherent in disorder. We have emerged from chaos through a series of happy accidents, but in an engineered culture it will be "impossible for the unplanned to erupt again." But there is no virtue in the accidental character of an accident, and the diversity which arises from disorder can not only be duplicated by design but also vastly extended. The experimental method is superior to simple observation just because it multiplies "accidents" in a systematic coverage of the possibilities. Technology offers many familiar examples. We no longer wait for immunity to disease to develop from a series of accidental exposures, nor do we wait for natural mutations in sheep and cotton to produce better fibers; but we continue to make use of such accidents when they occur, and we certainly do not prevent them. Many of the things we value have emerged from the clash of ignorant armies on darkling plains, but it is not therefore wise to encourage ignorance and darkness.

It is not always disorder itself which we are told we shall miss but certain admirable qualities in men which flourish only in the presence of disorder. A man rises above an unpropitious childhood to a position of eminence, and since we cannot give a plausible account of the action of so complex an environment, we attribute the achievement to some admirable faculty in the man himself. But such "faculties" are suspiciously like the explanatory fictions against which the history of science warns us. We admire Lincoln for rising above a deficient school system, but it was not necessarily something *in him* which permitted him to become an educated man in spite of it. His educational environment was certainly unplanned, but it could nevertheless have made a full contribution to his mature behavior. He was a rare man, but the circumstances of his childhood were rare too. We do not give Franklin Delano Roosevelt

the same credit for becoming an educated man with the help of
Groton and Harvard, although the same behavioral processes may
have been involved. The founding of Groton and Harvard somewhat reduced the possibility that fortuitous combinations of circumstances would erupt to produce other Lincolns. Yet the founders
can hardly be condemned for attacking an admirable human quality.

Another predicted consequence of a science of man is an excessive uniformity. We are told that effective control — whether governmental, religious, educational, economic, or social — will produce a race of men who differ from each other only through relatively refractory genetic differences. That would probably be bad
design, but we must admit that we are not now pursuing another
course from choice. In a modern school, for example, there is usually
a syllabus which specifies what every student is to learn by the end
of each year. This would be flagrant regimentation if anyone expected every student to comply. But some will be poor in particular
subjects, others will not study, others will not remember what they
have been taught, and diversity is assured. Suppose, however, that
we someday possess such effective educational techniques that every
student will in fact be put in possession of all the behavior specified
in a syllabus. At the end of the year, all students will correctly
answer all questions on the final examination and "must all have
prizes." Shoud we reject such a system on the grounds that in
making all students excellent it has made them all alike? Advocates
of the theory of a special faculty might contend that an important
advantage of the present system is that the good student learns *in*
spite of a system which is so defective that it is currently producing
bad students as well. But if really effective techniques are available,
we cannot avoid the problem of design simply by preferring the
status quo. At what point should education be deliberately inefficient?

Such predictions of the havoc to be wreaked by the application
of science to human affairs are usually made with surprising confidence. They not only show a faith in the orderliness of human behavior; they presuppose an established body of knowledge with the
help of which it can be positively asserted that the changes which
scientists propose to make will have quite specific results — albeit

not the results they foresee. But the predictions made by the critics of science must be held to be equally fallible and subject also to empirical test. We may be sure that many steps in the scientific design of cultural patterns will produce unforeseen consequences. But there is only one way to find out. And the test must be made, for if we cannot advance in the design of cultural patterns with absolute certainty, neither can we rest completely confident of the superiority of the status quo.

VI

Apart from their possibly objectionable consequences, scientific methods seem to make no provision for certain admirable qualities and faculties which seem to have flourished in less explicitly planned cultures; hence they are called "degrading" or "lacking in dignity." (Mr. Krutch has called the author's *Walden Two* an "ignoble Utopia.") The conditioned reflex is the current whipping boy. Because conditioned reflexes may be demonstrated in animals, they are spoken of as though they were exclusively subhuman. It is implied. as we have seen, that no behavioral processes are involved in education and moral discourse or, at least, that the processes are exclusively human. But men do show conditioned reflexes (when, for example, they are frightened by all instances of the control of human behavior because some instances engender fear), and animals do show processes similar to the human behavior involved in instruction and moral discourse. When Mr. Krutch asserts that " 'Conditioning' is achieved by methods which by-pass or, as it were, short-circuit those very reasoning faculties which education proposes to cultivate and exercise," he is making a technical statement which needs a definition of terms and a great deal of supporting evidence.

If such methods are called "ignoble" simply because they leave no room for certain admirable attributes, then perhaps the practice of admiration needs to be examined. We might say that the child whose education has been skillfully planned has been deprived of the right to intellectual heroism. Nothing has been left to be admired in the way he acquires an education. Similarly, we can conceive of moral training which is so adequate to the demands of the culture that men will be good practically automatically, but to that extent they will be deprived of the right to moral heroism, since we seldom admire automatic goodness. Yet if we consider the end of morals rather than certain virtuous means, is not "automatic goodness" a desirable state of affairs? Is it not, for example, the avowed goal of religious education? T. H. Huxley answered the question unambiguously: "If some great power would agree to make me always think what is true and do what is right, on condition of being a sort of clock and wound up every morning before I got out of bed, I should close instantly with the offer." Yet Mr. Krutch quotes this as the scarcely credible point of view of a "proto-modern" and seems himself to share T. S. Eliot's contempt for "... systems so perfect / That no one will need to be good."

"Having to be good" is an excellent example of an expendable honorific. It is inseparable from a particular form of ethical and moral control. We distinguish between the things we *have* to do to avoid punishment and those we *want* to do for rewarding consequences. In a culture which did not resort to punishment we should never "have" to do anything except with respect to the punishing contingencies which arise directly in the physical environment. And we are moving toward such a culture, because the neurotic, not to say psychotic, by-products of control through punishment have long since led compassionate men to seek alternative techniques. Recent research has explained some of the objectionable results of punishment and has revealed resources of at least equal power in "positive reinforcement." It is reasonable to look forward to a time when man will seldom "have" to do anything, although he may show interest, energy, imagination, and productivity far beyond the level seen under the present system (except for rare eruptions of the unplanned).

What we have to do we do with *effort*. We call it "work." There is no other way to distinguish between exhausting labor and the possibly equally energetic but rewarding activity of play. It is presumably good cultural design to replace the former with the latter. But an adjustment in attitudes is needed. We are much more practiced in admiring the heroic labor of a Hercules than the activity of one who works without having to. In a truly effective educational system the student might not "have to work" at all, but that possibility is likely to be received by the contemporary teacher with an emotion little short of rage.

We cannot reconcile traditional and scientific views by agreeing upon *what* is to be admired or condemned. The question is whether anything is to be so treated. Praise and blame are cultural practices which have been adjuncts of the prevailing system of control in Western democracy. All peoples do not engage in them for the same purposes or to the same extent, nor, of course, are the same behaviors always classified in the same way as subject to praise or blame. In admiring intellectual and moral heroism and unrewarding labor, and in rejecting a world in which these would be uncommon, we are simply demonstrating our own cultural conditioning. By promoting certain tendencies to admire and censure, the group of which we are a part has arranged for the social reinforcement and punishment needed to assure a high level of intellectual and moral industry. Under other and possibly better controlling systems, the behavior which we now admire would occur, but not under those conditions which make it admirable, and we should have no reason to admire it because the culture would have arranged for its maintenance in other ways.

To those who are stimulated by the glamorous heroism of the battlefield, a peaceful world may not be a better world. Others may reject a world without sorrow, longing, or a sense of guilt because the relevance of deeply moving works of art would be lost. To many who have devoted their lives to the struggle to be wise and good, a world without confusion and evil might be an empty thing. A nostalgic concern for the decline of moral heroism has been a dominating theme in the work of Aldous Huxley. In *Brave New World* he could see in the application of science to human affairs only a travesty on the notion of the Good (just as George Orwell, in *1984*, could foresee nothing but horror). In a recent issue of *Esquire*, Huxley has expressed the point this way: "We have had religious revolutions, we have had political, industrial, economic and nationalistic revolutions. All of them, as our descendants will discover, were but ripples in an ocean of conservatism — trivial by comparison with the psychological revolution toward which we are so rapidly moving. *That* will really be a revolution. When it is over, the human race will give no further trouble." (Footnote for the reader of the future: This was not meant as a happy ending. Up to 1956 men had been admired, if at all, either for causing trouble or alleviating it. Therefore —.)

It will be a long time before the world can dispense with heroes and hence with the cultural practice of admiring heroism, but we move in that direction whenever we act to prevent war, famine, pestilence, and disaster. It will be a long time before man will never need to submit to punishing environments or engage in exhausting labor, but we move in that direction whenever we make food, shelter, clothing, and labor-saving devices more readily available. We may mourn the passing of heroes but not the conditions which make for heroism. We can spare the self-made saint or sage as we spare the laundress on the river's bank struggling against fearful odds to achieve cleanliness.

VII

The two great dangers in modern democratic thinking are illustrated in a paper by former Secretary of State Dean Acheson. "For a long time now," writes Mr. Acheson, "we have gone along with some well-tested principles of conduct: That it was better to tell the truth than falsehoods; ... that duties were older than and as fundamental as rights; that, as Justice Holmes put it, the mode by which the inevitable came to pass was effort; that to perpetrate a harm was wrong no matter how many joined in it ... and so on.... Our institutions are founded on the assumption that most people follow these principles most of the time because they want to, and the institutions work pretty well when this assumption is true. More recently, however, bright people have been fooling with the machinery in the human head and they have discovered quite a lot.... Hitler introduced new refinements [as the result of which] a whole people have been utterly confused and corrupted. Unhappily neither the possession of this knowledge nor the desire to use it was confined to Hitler.... Others dip from this same devil's cauldron."

The first dangerous notion in this passage is that most people follow democratic principles of conduct "because they want to." This does not account for democracy or any other form of government if we have not explained why people *want* to behave in given ways. Although it is tempting to assume that it is human nature to believe in democratic principles, we must not overlook the "cultural engineering" which produced and continues to maintain democratic practices. If we neglect the conditions which produce democratic *behavior,* it is useless to try to maintain a democratic *form* of government. And we cannot expect to export a democratic form of government successfully if we do not also provide for the cultural practices which will sustain it. Our forebears did not discover the essential nature of man; they evolved a pattern of behavior which worked remarkably well under the circumstances. The "set of principles" expressed in that pattern is not the only true set or necessarily the best. Mr. Acheson has presumably listed the most unassailable items; some of them are probably beyond question, but others — concerning duty and effort — may need revision as the world changes.

The second — and greater — threat to the democracy which Mr. Acheson is defending is his assumption that knowledge is necessarily on the side of evil. All the admirable things he mentions are attributed to the innate goodness of man, all the detestable to "fooling with the machinery in the human head." This is reminiscent of the position, taken by other institutions engaged in the control of men, that certain forms of knowledge are in themselves evil. But how out of place in a democratic philosophy! Have we come this far only to conclude that well-intentioned people cannot study the behavior of men without becoming tyrants or that informed men cannot show good will? Let us for once have strength and good will on the same side.

VIII

Far from being a threat to the tradition of Western democracy, the growth of a science of man is a consistent and probably inevitable part of it. In turning to the external conditions which shape and maintain the behavior of men, while questioning the reality of inner qualities and faculties to which human achievements were once attributed, we turn from the ill-defined and remote to the observable and manipulable. Though it is a painful step, it has far-reaching consequences, for it not only sets higher standards of human welfare but shows us how to meet them. A change in a theory of human nature cannot change the facts. The achievements of man in science, art, literature, music, and morals will survive any interpretation we place upon them. The uniqueness of the individual is unchallenged in the scientific view. Man, in short, will remain man. (There will be much to admire for those who are so inclined. Possibly the noblest achievement to which man can aspire, even according to present standards, is to accept himself for what he is, as that is revealed to him by the methods which he devised and tested on a part of the world in which he had only a small personal stake.)

If Western democracy does not lose sight of the aims of humanitarian action, it will welcome the almost fabulous support of its own science of man and will strengthen itself and play an important role in building a better world for everyone. But if it cannot put its "democratic philosophy" into proper historical perspective — if, under the control of attitudes and emotions which it generated for other purposes, it now rejects the help of science — then it must be prepared for defeat. For if we continue to insist that science has nothing to offer but a new and more horrible form of tyranny, we may produce just such a result by allowing the strength of science to fall into the hands of despots. And if, with luck, it were to fall instead to men of good will in other political communities, it would be perhaps a more ignominious defeat; for we should then, through a miscarriage of democratic principles, be forced to leave to others the next step in man's long struggle to control nature and himself.

4 : *The Cult of Efficiency*

Christopher Jencks

The Rise of the Meritocracy, like *Brave New World,* describes a utopia, although the former uses the guise of history, while the latter purports to be a novel. Both utopias are seductive because they carry a contemporary ideal to its logical, if distant, conclusion. Thus Huxley's world is the fruition of the cult of happiness, while Michael Young's derives from the cult of efficiency.

Young describes the world of 2034 A.D., in which ceaseless international economic competition has led to ever greater demands for efficient production. As a result, society has deified "intelligence," by which it means the ability to solve production problems. The result is that the intellectual, educational, and social elites become coterminous. The "intelligent" people who contribute the most to social efficiency and productivity constitute an aristocracy, while the less effective workers are reduced to proletarian status. This system of stratification is peculiarly stable because all the proletarians with enough brain to know how and why they are oppressed are

From *The New Republic,* September 7, 1959, p. 18. Copyright 1959, Harrison-Blaine of New Jersey, Inc.

systematically drafted into the elite. And the seeming necessity and logic of the cult of intelligence prevents them from modifying the system which has so rewarded them. But something is missing, and the utopias which embody these values turn out to be gruesome anti-utopias. How can this be? What can be wrong with a world in which people are happy, or a world which is run intelligently? Certainly neither author is prepared to make an open case for misery or stupidity.

Huxley's critique of happiness does draw to some extent upon his reader's masochism, playing up the sweetness of temporary deprivation. But in large part, he taps reservoirs of religious and artistic values, employing ideologies of virtue and creativity to attack the ideology of happiness. The conflict is neatly dramatized by making the hero embody the deviant values, and while he is overwhelmed in the end, presumably the reader who identifies with him is not.

Young's critique of meritocracy is subtler. He presents the book from the viewpoint of a social historian, trying to explain perplexing unrest among the working class in the year 2033. This fictitious author identifies with the intelligentsia, and he encourages the reader to do the same. The conflict is summed up by a "Worker's Manifesto": "Were we to evaluate people not only according to their intelligence and their education, their occupation and their power, but according to their kindness and their courage, their imagination and sensitivity, their sympathy and generosity, there could be no classes." This is the ethical and historical issue in *Meritocracy,* brilliantly dramatized by the whole meticulous fantasy. Yet when we have followed Young through 160 pages to this denouement, we may yet find his position untenable.

From the ethical viewpoint, we must ask whether we ought to expect social structure to reward all the virtues which a civilization deems important. Perhaps other institutions (such as the family) can be expected to encourage such things as generosity and sensitivity; these virtues may even become corrupted when they become vehicles to social mobility and status. Perhaps society *should* confine itself to self-perpetuation, by rewarding only those virtues which lead to economic productivity or administrative skill.

A second ethical question is whether any scheme of "evaluation" can lead to a classless society, no matter how numerous the "valuable" qualities. This truly horrifying form of stratification may be the logical consequences of naive egalitarianism (which assumes that by exercising our ingenuity we can discover equal merit in all people, and thus a basis for mutual respect). Perhaps a truly classless society cannot be founded on justice, but only on compassion — the recognition that while people are not equally meritorious, they are equally deserving.

If we turn from moral to historical ambiguities in *Meritocracy,* the question is whether we are actually moving toward an intellectual elite. In art, the answer must be affirmative. The powerful are getting more educated, and the educated are getting more powerful. But if we ask whether this means that the power elite is more "intelligent," the question becomes ambiguous. Look, for example, at two tendencies in America. First, children who cannot do the work in school are usually promoted anyway. This means that practically any persevering youth who can adapt to classroom mores can get a degree. To a lesser extent the same applies to college. In other words, raw intelligence — feats of memory, etc. — is becoming less important than ability to adapt to the middle class culture which educators impose and reward. Then too, look at business. Where once skill was important, now personality is emphasized. Though we suffer from a shortage of skilled personnel, we are already screening them with personality tests as well as IQ tests. "Intelligence" is coming to mean ability to solve human problems as well as economic-material ones, ability to manipulate (and be manipulated by) people, rather than objects. This may be a mixed blessing, but it means more rather than less emphasis on such "human" virtues as sensitivity, generosity, sympathy and imagination.

Perhaps, then, the drift is away from the meritocracy Young fears, rather than toward it. If we are entering an automation-world in which production will take care of itself, with minimal management and effort, then perhaps we are also entering a world which can afford such vices and virtues as stinginess and generosity, obtuseness and sensitivity, cruelty and kindness. And if this is true, tomorrow's society will not be more egalitarian (because the "human" virtues are no more evenly distributed than intelligence), but neither will it be the rigid meritocracy that Young fears.

5: The Anti-Utopia of the Twentieth Century

Eugen Weber

There is a passage in the works of Berdyaev which Aldous Huxley uses to introduce his novel, *Brave New World* — a passage in which the philosopher points out that Utopias appear far more possible today than they ever did before. The issue now, says Berdyaev, is not how to realize Utopia, but how to prevent its realization — how to oppose the constant developments in directions that were, until quite recently, still considered utopian; how to check further advances toward a state of things which certain thinkers coninue to present by means of the utopian convention as something that is to be desired. One consequence of this conception is the anti-Utopian novel, which uses the familiar utopian convention to express a mood of dread and despair occasioned by the results or the implications of utopian dreams.

Historically speaking, this is a new attitude. Until recently utopian schemes excited approval or disapproval but seldom, if ever, fear or the bitter opposition that a feeling of immediate danger can

From *The South Atlantic Quarterly*, vol. 58 (Summer 1959), pp. 440-447.

beget. The utopian form traditionally eschewed the notion of reality or immediacy. Utopia was nowhere, or it was very far away. Now, this is no longer so; Utopia is with us, or just around the corner, and it generates reactions based on quite concrete hopes or fears. It is quite significant that, whereas the classic Utopia stands in a sort of never-never land, out of time and space, the anti-utopian novel of recent years has been brought closer and closer to us, not so much, one would say, to foster an added sense of reality in the reader, as to reflect the sense of impending doom in the writer. Koestler's *Age of Longing* is placed in the fifties; and so is the third world war that breaks out at the end of Virgil Gheorghiu's *Twenty-fifth Hour*. Orwell's *1984* is for the day after tomorrow. It is not so widely known that another utopian novel exists, also placed in 1984 — *The Napoleon of Notting Hill*, by G. K. Chesterton. But Chesterton's picture of 1984 is a fantasy; Orwell's is a deliberate projection of the immediate present into what is presented as the immediate future. Even Aldous Huxley (who, in 1931, had dated his *Brave New World* six hundred years hence) explains in a foreword of 1946 that "today it seems quite possible that the horror may be upon us within a single century." Accordingly, *Ape and Essence*, which he published in 1948, deals with a period much closer to our own.

The utopian novel, as a literary form, has proved an excellent vehicle for concepts of "The Good Life" or "The Good Society"; or again for criticism of the existing society by caricature or dissection of current practices and concepts in the sort of satire with which we are familiar through the works of Swift and Voltaire. The anti-Utopia characteristic of our own century might be considered as a subdivision of utopian satire. Yet it is peculiar to itself and particularized by the fact that, whilst it sometimes attacks existing societies or systems as such, it also and just as frequently attacks utopian ideals, or what may appear as their fulfillment.

The anti-utopians recognize in the society which they criticize the fulfillment of the dreams of yesterday. Lewis Mumford in his *Story of Utopias* exaggerates when he writes of nineteenth-century Utopias as being "all machinery," but he is not far off. The anti-utopians have seen the triumph of machinery, of automation, of rational development, of the general over the particular. As they see it, Utopia stands for the unreal against the real, for the technique against the man, for the rational against the many-sided human. With all its superficial materialism, its essence (as Gabriel Marcel points out in his Introduction to *The Twenty-fifth Hour*) is the substitution of abstract for concrete, the sacrifice of the real for the ideal. And the result of this development is the theme of Gheorghiu's work: the world no longer belongs to men; it belongs to "the process," it belongs to "the machine" that has taken over. Men are ciphers, their fates inscribed in advance on the punch cards of a gigantic IBM machine. It is the procrustean world of Aldous Huxley, "made up by scientists — if mankind does not fit, too bad for mankind!" It is the robot world of Karel Capek, in which mankind succumbs before Rossum's universal robots, first created to serve it.

In this, as in other respects, Utopias and anti-Utopias reflect the great debate of our time — how to reconcile direction with freedom, free enterprise with a planned society. A recent utopian novel, *Walden Two*, written by a well-known psychologist, B. F. Skinner, suggests that such questions are spurious and out-of-date, that they are no more, in fact, than "pseudo-questions of linguistic origin." "Our members are practically always doing what they want to do," says the planner of Walden Two, "but we see to it that they will want to do precisely the things which are best for themselves and for the community." The only way to achieve freedom in Walden Two is by an illusion of freedom. According to this view, freedom docs not belong in the good society; it is no more than a conditioned reflex.

The eventual possibility of such a state of things is corroborated by reports of current achievement in the field of behavioral engineering and biocontrol. Rossum's universal robots may have been good enough for the twenties, but by October, 1956, the National Electronics Conference in Chicago could consider the prospect of biocontrol, defined as "the control of physical movements, mental processes, emotional reactions and apparent sensory perceptions...by means of bioelectrical signals which are injected into the central nervous system of the subject." Perhaps, as Winston Smith eventually learns to admit, "Freedom *is* Slavery"; and perhaps biocontrolled slavery is the nearest approach to freedom that our time can expect. However, it is not surprising that, with such ominous prospects before them, with realities almost as ominous around them, and with Utopias like *Walden Two* to provoke them, the anti-utopian writers feel that they are dealing with present problems and present dangers which affect them and their readers with an immediacy that never existed before.

That is why their work reflects the kind of disillusion and fear for which there would have been no material basis in another age. Until the twentieth century, no large-scale attempts had been made to carry out utopian concepts. There was the abortive reign of the Anabaptists in Münster; there were the programs of the Enlightened Despots — limited in scope and even more so in achievement. But their failure was never the failure of the utopian dream itself: no one ever defaced Cythera, because the right ship for it never sailed. And, in any case, Cythera was always somewhere else. In this connection, it is interesting to see how, in earlier utopian satires, the horror is localized — either in time (as when Jack London implies a later, better, world from which the story of the *Iron Heel* dictatorship is told), or in space (as in the Third Book of *Gulliver's Travels,* or in Condé B. Pallen's *Crucible Island,* which is the account of an escape from a socialist dictatorship on a distant island).

But in 1918, a year before *Crucible Island* appeared, an Englishman, Owen Gregory, published *Meccania — the Super-State,* the apprehensively bitter caricature of a totalitarian police-state isolated from the rest of the world in concentration-camp-like horror. *Meccania,* which refers to Germany, may seem somewhat premature, though prophetic, and it still allows a possibility of escape. But the sense of doom so characteristic of later works is already there: "It seemed not impossible," writes the visitor who has left Meccania, "that the nightmare I had escaped from was a doom impending over the whole world.... I could not dismiss this doubt...." Very soon, what was doubt for Owen Gregory appears with certainty in the work of Edward Shanks, Karel Capek, and Eugene Zamiatin. In

R.U.R. (1923) and *We* (1924) escape is hardly conceivable; the utterness of human defeat is insured by the heights of human ingenuity. In *The People of the Ruins,* a more obscure book published in 1920, Edward Shanks predicts social revolution in England for 1924, as a prelude to a century and a half of war and decay for the world. As the book ends, the hero (who has straddled the twentieth- and twenty-first centuries by a typical utopian device) has "a vision of the world sinking further below the point from which in his youth he had seen it.... Cities would be burnt, bridges broken down, tall towers destroyed and all the wealth and learning of humanity would shiver to a few shards and a little dust." But the horror-image of 1920 is still jejune, the subtly-tortured fates of *1984* are not yet, and the hero simply shoots himself over the corpse of his beloved.

Through all these works echoes the mood that Paul Valéry expressed in *Variété* in 1919 in his famous reflections on the European crisis: "Nous autres, civilizations, nous savons maintenant que nous sommes mortelles...." We are mortal; history is not simply the tale of human progress; the divine machine can and will run down. It was a hard awakening and a hard admission to make, after the high dreams of the eighteenth and nineteenth centuries.

Perhaps, after all, it is the failure of eighteenth-century rationalism and of its dreams that we mourn today, but the significant thing is that until today we could not be sure. Every partial failure, every shot at perfection that missed, merely turned the eyes of men toward another panacea, toward another pattern, toward another plan. Nor is this over. But our generation has seen so many hopes arise only to be broken, that every utopian illusion (Russian, Nazi, British, American, technological, and psychological) has furnished its quota of disillusioned anti-Utopias. Theirs is not a romantic utopianism, yearning back toward a golden age or toward a simpler primitive life. The Savage in *Brave New World* is no more attractive than his more advanced contemporaries. And, of course, they know better than to offer one more panacea in lieu of the others that have failed. This is what makes them not just opponents of one utopian pattern, but opponents of the utopian heresy itself.

For them there can be no salvation by legislation. They point out how, in trying to make man and society perfect, the utopian has twisted both into a gruesome shape. They see the triumph of the artificial world which the old Utopias preconized and which their contemporary imitations enforce — they see this triumph as the defeat of humanity and the defeat of man. Under such conditions Order means regimentation, Content means conditioning, Education means indoctrination, Freedom is only a conditioned reflex. The new security and social discipline appears as those of the concentration camp — potential in concepts like those presented in *Walden Two,* actual in the work of Gregory, Zamiatin, Fialko (*The New City,* 1937), and Orwell. This actualization of the potential, both of Utopia and of real life, is characteristic of anti-Utopias as it is of our time. Nowadays, what Daniel Halévy has called "the acceleration of history" allows illusion to become disillusion within a very short period. So, what used to be a dream (in Russia, or Germany, or America) has become a nightmare, a fact which makes the anti-utopian afraid and, like any man awakened from a nightmare, reluctant to return to any dreams. More than mere disillusion with existing conditions and aspirations, the anti-utopian expresses the conviction that there is no hope elsewhere, no hope in what must be only variations on the same theme. The utopian is either a hopeful critic or a hopeful rebel, because he has an alternative to offer; and even such bitter utopian satires as *The Iron Heel* still sound a note of hope. The anti-utopian does not believe in alternatives: it is too late for that. He is defeated before he starts to write. That is why we find him at his most typical in Europe, where disillusion can be most thoroughly experienced, where the utmost awareness might be expected of the implications and results of utopian reforms. Americans are not yet really disillusioned with the possibilities open to them in the political field. They have produced utopian satires of the bitterest kind — D. N. Keller, *Revolt of the Pedestrians;* Ward Moore, *Greener than Grass;* S. Mead, *The Great Ball of Wax* — but the dread and despair characteristic of anti-Utopia appear only in the work of the "technologists" — Bradbury, Vonnegut, Azimov, etc., writers who see the machines taking over; human personality, initiative, and fantasy lost or floundering

in a sea of gadgets, experience garnered vicariously through electronic apparatus; independence surrendered or abolished for a mess
of conditioned security. The mood of the American anti-Utopia is
just as despairing, the defeat of the individual is just as sure, but
the end is attained by different means in plot and in treatment, which
themselves reflect the author's different experience. Even so, American anti-Utopias are relatively recent, rare, and significantly cam-
ouflaged behind the appropriate but conveniently protective apparatus of science-fiction.

From our point of view, the formative period of anti-utopianism
lies in the years following the First World War, when the high
hopes of former times, culminating in 1917 and 1918, were seen to
be left unfulfilled. A spate of "political" anti-Utopias reflects this
disillusion through the twenties and it is reinforced in the thirties
by several attacks against the Utopia of the Nazis. A second war-
period of hope and sometimes desperate endeavor, 1939-1945, was
marked by the absence of pessimistic works (apart from a propa-
gandistic reissue of Constantine's *Swastika Night,* first published
in 1937) until, in August 1945, George Orwell's *Animal Farm* opened
a new series of attacks on popular illusions. But, though the next
few years saw the publication of the great classics of the *genre*
(*1984* and the *Twenty-fifth Hour,* 1949, and *The Age of Longing,*
1951), a more significant phenomenon of the postwar decade was the
appearance of the "technical" anti-Utopias which had been almost
entirely absent before the war. *Brave New World* (1931) and,
stretching a point, the work of Karel Capek, were almost alone of
their kind in the earlier period. With Huxley's *Ape and Essence,*
however, anti-utopian literature began to reflect a growing concern
for man in his struggle against the results of his own technical
ingenuity.

"The true poet," Goethe has said, "is only a masked father con-
fessor, whose special function it is to exhibit what is dangerous in
sentiment and pernicious in action by a vivid picture of their consequences." In the pursuit of this task, political anti-Utopias find it
increasingly hard to compete with the daily press and with the many
accounts of prisoners escaped or released from the concentration-

camp worlds of contemporary Utopias. But, in the guise of science-fiction or of utopian satire, the technologists take their place. The inhuman society which they portray is a newer, more up-to-date version of *R.U.R.*, but without the gleam of hope which was never absent from the work of the Czech journalist. Significantly enough, the authors of this new school are all American by birth or adoption, whereas their political-minded predecessors or contemporaries tend to be Europeans.

Insofar as the anti-utopian allows us a glimmer of hope, it lies in the instincts, in fantasy, in the irrational, in the peculiarly individualistic and egotistic characteristics most likely to shatter any system or order. This accounts for the importance of basic feelings — sex, love, selfishness, fantasy — which all utopian planners try to control and in which all anti-utopians seem to put their faith, insofar as they have any faith. Again and again, like Ray Bradbury in his remarkable short story, *Usher II,* the anti-utopian calls on the irrational to disrupt and destroy the planned order. Nor does it matter very much what the order is: "New presbyter is but old priest writ large." The intention is to shun systems and orders altogether, to assert the lonely individual against a society too satisfied with itself, its ends and its means. In this sense, the anti-uopians are the Surrealists of our time. The main aim of the Surrealists, Maurice Nadeau tells us, "was to make men despair of themselves and of society." The anti-Utopia of the Surrealists preached the gospel of absolute revolt, total insubmission, sabotage of institutions and of social order. Like a later generation operating round St. Germain des Prés, they felt that it was up to them to show up society, to emphasize the absurdity of its organization and its value, in order to free the individual. Their failure is a document of sorts, and so is the restatement of this part of their doctrine in later years at the hands of popular novelists.

Yet, if the anti-utopians are eager to reassert neglected human values, we must not forget that, in a sense, the Utopia is the characteristic manifestation of the Western cultural tradition. The search for order, the drive to harness nature and eliminate the unpredictable, are eminently human and peculiarly Western. The presumption of man, always biting off more of the fruit of the tree of knowledge than he can chew, is a stock mythological situation. Just as traditionally, his pride goes before a fall: he reaches to the sky and his tower topples over; he tries to be godlike and is chained to a rock or cast out of Eden. The Church is familiar with the heresy that man can build a paradise on earth, and it condemns over and over again the utopian heresy, the idea that a good society can be shaped according to the concepts of human reason. Obviously, our anti-utopian friends are on the side of the angels, or at least on the side of the Church. Where Utopia expresses the ambitious temerity, anti-Utopian stresses the Fall. Thus, in Isaac Asimov's novel, *The End of Eternity* (1955), men have acquired control of Eternity and find themselves at last to be the masters of their fate. But they cannot deny with impunity those mysterious and uncontrollable elements that make for failure; another Adam is tempted by another Eve and man is expelled from Eternity as he was from Eden.

And so, over and over again, the anti-utopian warns against tinkering with nature and prophesies failure and doom for those who persist. Yet this very antithetic character of his work indicates its close connection with the thesis it attacks: to plan and to despair are both reasonable, both human. Utopia and anti-Utopia are the strophe and antistrophe of a chorus constantly commenting on the doings of man. They continue the long debate between society and the individual, order and anarchy, affirmation and denial, every one of these dangerous if pressed too far and needing an antithesis just as potentially violent.

It is not surprising, therefore, that an age which has grown disillusioned with the omnipotence of human reason and the results of utopian presumption should produce the anti-Utopia: a literature of disillusion, no mere statement of irrationalistic denial, but deeply skeptical and aware that dreams — if pressed too far — lead either to nightmares or to frustrated waking.

6: Utopianism and Politics

J. L. Talmon

I feel the more honored by the invitation to address this Summer School for not being a Tory. In the words used by Burke to describe the British Constitution, the Tory Party is an inheritance solely and exclusively belonging to the people of this country, while I am only an occasional visitor to these shores, gratefully enjoying liberal hospitality. I may, however, as an Israeli claim to be part of a conservative tradition of immemorial antiquity. For indeed it would be difficult to find a more eloquent testimony to the strength of conservatism than the allegiance of countless Jewish generations to a tradition which was in no position to employ coercion to exact adherence, the observance of which was often fraught with grave disadvantages and sometimes peril, and the identity of which has at all times been subject to powerful solvents from outside.

My theme is Utopianism and Politics. Since the time of the French Revolution, a substantial proportion of the most politically

From *Utopianism and Politics* (London: Conservative Political Centre, 1957).

conscious and active people have tended to equate Politics with Utopianism. Yet the two are, in essence, quite different. Politics I would define, in Aristotelian terms, as the art of husbandry, the technique of administering a State conceived of as being an enlarged household. It has often been said that Politics involves a choice between evils or, more charitably, an acceptance of the second best. This is because Politics is concerned with very intractable material — and by that, I mean men. And it is not only men who have to be administered. It is also men who are engaged in permanent debate as to how and by whom the task should be carried out. In this sense Politics is of course a struggle for power, and thus charged with an ambivalence which can hardly ever be resolved by any attempt to apportion the share of disinterested conviction and the part of the urge for power that respectively go to make a statesman and to shape a policy decision. The two are so intertwined that the cynic who can see only naked ambition and the naive doctrinaire who acknowledges only principles incarnate will prove equally wrong.

Utopianism, on the other hand, signifies that one assumes as possible (or even expects as inevitable) an ultimate condition of absolute harmony in which individual self-expression and social cohesion, though seemingly incompatible, will be combined. In other words, Politics is concerned with the careful manipulation of concrete data of experience, by reference to the logic and to the limitations inherent in any given historical situation; whereas Utopianism postulates a definite goal or preordained finale to history, for the attainment of which you need to recast and remold all aspects of life and society in accordance with some very explicit principle. It could be said that while starting out with the wish to secure to man the means of full self-expression, Utopianism ends with a determination to impose a wholly impersonal pattern. It tends in other words to replace history by sociology. The tragedy is that any principle must be embodied in men. The higher the validity claimed for the objective pattern, the wider the powers and the fewer the men to whom these powers may be granted.

Before the late eighteenth century, the Utopian approach was confined to literary exercises — social satires and allegories — or to the life of relatively small societies or sects of extreme *exaltés*. Then it won dominance, or at least wide currency, on the continent of Europe and became there, in a variety of ways, the common denominator of Socialist, Communist, and kindred schools of political thought. Why did this change take place when it did?

In the first place, because in the age of absolutism or of government by hereditary privileged groups, those at the helm were concerned primarily with keeping order and upholding the prestige of the country in the world; rather with preventing discontent than with making the peoples free and happy. The peoples then — it will be said — decided to shake off tutelage and be masters of their own fate and makers of their own salvation. It seems to me however that these changes and the factors that brought them about are not in themselves enough to account for the emergence of Utopianism in political life.

The decisive factor was, I think, the decline of the religious sanction, and in particular the decline of belief in the doctrine of Original Sin. I am not concerned with the theological validity of this doctrine, but I do believe it to contain an extremely important psychological truth. It stands for the terrific mystery summed up in the words: "Video meliora proboque, Deteriora sequor," I know and respect what is right, but I do what is wrong. It teaches us that evil actions are due, not necessarily to lack of knowledge, but rather to some failure of will, some defect in the mechanism of man, some "weakness of our mortal nature." Now once this doctrine is taken for granted, one accepts without question a clear distinction between theory and practice, between what should be and what can be, between private morality based on Natural Law and political morality which is vitiated by the persistence of evil in human nature, between (if you like) Church and State, Heaven and earth. The conclusion then is clear: that man and society will never be able to save themselves solely by their own exertions, but that grace, coming from above or outside, is needed for salvation. Furthermore, men's unruly and weak nature requires government from above, by a God-appointed Church, Divine Right of Kings, an aristocracy, or — in more abstract terms — ancient traditions, deep-seated beliefs, fixed habits.

With the ushering in of the Age of Reason there emerged and grew in intensity a belief that man was by nature good, or at least perfectible. The natural urges of man were good, and if given a free rein, would set themselves into a pattern of harmony. A rational order was calculated to ensure a harmonious reconciliation of all interests. The cohesive structure of the universe was, in brief, a guarantee that if all impediments to self-expression were removed, a state of absolute justice based on the supremacy of reason could and would be achieved.

The doctrine of Original Sin was denounced as a conspiracy by forces of exploitation and oppression. It was held to be an important argument in favor of the claim that the people are in need of superiors to keep them down. Repressive policies, it was said, diverted the energy of the natural impulses into channels of anti-social perversion, which strengthened still more the pretensions of the ruling orders.

With the decline of religious faith the problem which the Prophet defined in the Bible, "Wherefore doth the way of the wicked prosper?" received a new interpretation. Before, the question could be considered on the transcendental plane: one had the assurance that the account would be settled in the hereafter, in another place. Once religious belief was undermined, however, the evils and injustices of this life could no longer be regarded as merely temporary or temporal; therefore, they ceased to be tolerable, and men began to put their faith in the achievement of perfect justice and the settling of accounts in this world, not the next.

It is true that the right of resistance to temporal rulers is very ancient, and that tyrannicide has often had the vehement approval of theologians. But from the late eighteenth century onward, all this took on a completely new character. Men now rose in arms, not to burn, kill, and ravage in a kind of elemental *chagrin,* but to effect in society some revolutionary transformation; not to correct a specific social evil, but to abolish evil itself. Every riot or rebellion seemed to be accompanied by a bell tolling for the Day of Judgment;

and when the Industrial Revolution began to overwhelm an unprepared society with unprecedented problems, it was seen not as a
period of transient crisis but as an apocalyptic hour.

Men had been taught that they had a right to expect happiness
forthwith, and a series of great technological discoveries seemed to
have created instruments to ease man's toil and to satisfy his needs,
while industrial organization and division of labor appeared to fore-
shadow a high degree of social cohesion. Instead of fulfilling these
hopes, the Industrial Revolution seemed at first to produce nothing
but evil: bondage to the machine, wretched misery and recurrent
crisis. It was as if the intentions of nature to bring salvation had
been willfully perverted by the intervention of some evil design.
And the conclusion suggested itself that a forceful intercession was
required to frustrate the evil forces and to lend a helping hand to
destiny to take its predetermined course.

The tragic paradox of Utopianism has been that instead of
bringing about, as it promised, a system of final and permanent
stability, it gave rise to utter restlessness, and in place of a reconciliation between human freedom and social cohesion, it brought
totalitarian coercion.

There is a nineteenth-century story of an Englishman inquiring at
a public library for the text of one of the French Constitutions and
being told, "We do not keep periodicals here." The fact that within
twenty-five years France experienced a succession and variety of
régimes, coups, and revolutions, destroyed the sense that there were
certain things that could be taken for granted, accepted as permanent facts of life. Hence the luxuriant crop of Utopian blueprints,
social and constitutional, presented as though the whole slate had
been wiped clean, as though you could start from scratch. Hence
also the terrible instability of political life and the violence of political warfare. For Utopianism is based upon the assumption that
reason alone — not habit, or tradition, or prejudice — can be the
sole criterion in human affairs. But the end of this assumption is
that reason, like mathematics, must command universal consent, since
it has sole and exclusive truth. In fact, reason turns out to be the
most fallible and precarious of guides; because there is nothing to

prevent a variety of "reasons" from cropping up, each claiming sole and exclusive validity, and between which there can be no compromise, no arbiter except force. To put it in another way: Utopianism postulates free self-expression by the individual and at the same time absolute social cohesion. This combination is possible only if all individuals agree. All individuals, however, do not agree. Therefore, if you expect unanimity, there is ultimately no escape from dictatorship. The individual must either be forced to agree, or his agreement must be engineered by some kind of fake plebiscite, or he must be treated as an outlaw, or traitor, or counterrevolutionary subversive, or whatever you will.

The great Swiss historian Jacob Burckhardt, a grim prophet of doom and not a very charitable person, pointed out how the notion that men were perfectible apart from the grace of God, and that Utopia here on earth was possible and almost inevitable, was bound to produce arrogantly presumptuous attitudes. Before this, men had felt that life was, to some extent, a sacrifice; certainly it demanded a spirit of service and duty. From now on, they began to think first and foremost, and sometimes exclusively, not of their duties but of their rights, not of what was due *from* them, but of what was due *to* them. They demanded a larger share, a "fair" share, an equal share; and since the quantity of things which can be distributed is limited, those whose expectations were disappointed were consumed by bitterness and envy and frustration. Hence, the decline of belief in the religious doctrine of Original Sin and the rise of belief in the secular doctrine of the Rights of Man, far from having produced happiness, in fact engendered misery, since it encouraged appetites that could never be satisfied.

At the same time, instead of serving as a challenge to nobler actions and greater humanity, the doctrine of the Rights of Man became a pretext for the pursuit of greater enjoyment, and nothing but enjoyment. Governments that were not fulfilling material expectations were abolished one after another by restless peoples. This provided the opportunity for demagogues and dictators to appear on the stage, promising a new Heaven and a new earth. Seeking to satisfy the material cravings which put them in power, they had to place an obsessive emphasis on higher production; and since, to achieve this, an appeal to idealism is rarely if ever enough, they had to induce people to work harder by offering them even more unequal rewards or by threatening them with very heavy punishments — in the Soviet context, Stakhanovism or Siberia. Lacking such legitimacy as comes from lineage, or even from the ballot box, they had to keep those whom they ruled together by thrills and stunts; and the most effective stunt of all, of course, is to create a war emergency, a pervasive sense of national peril.

As against the indubitable gains we have to set off the vast losses. If indeed we have achieved an unprecedentedly wide distribution of good things, mass production of shoddy standardized goods has killed the craftsman's pride in creative achievement. The huge crowds at Universities do not signify a growing thirst for learning, but a scramble for jobs and positions by a restless and dissatisfied academic *Lumpenproletariat.* Illiteracy has practically been abolished, but never have millions been treated to coarser vulgarity in print than now. A person may now travel more safely on the highway and be more certain of not being molested in the street after midnight. But of how little account is this higher degree of personal safety in comparison with the nightmare of total war, keeping in deadly grip the whole of mankind? We have learned to deal with epidemics and solved many problems thought previously insoluble, but the complexity of modern civilization has created problems which are too vast for the human intellect to comprehend and before which the ordinary man stands utterly baffled and wholly impotent. So much for Burckhardt's chilling criticisms of the modern *Weltanschauung,* based on the denial of Original Sin and the unshakable faith in progress, and represented by the advent of "the masses."

Returning to the more strictly political sphere, we come now to the essential difference between the Utopian approach and the English conservative approach — and, since I have the misfortune of not being English myself, may I indulge in the very un-English eccentricity of thinking of your conservative tradition as having two branches, a Tory branch and a Labour branch, the one a little more so, the other a little less so! Now the English Constitution, as Edmund Burke described it, is a "prescriptive" constitution, one "whose sole authority is that it has existed time out of mind." It is really based upon habits, upon a tradition of behavior, upon ways of feeling, upon implicit, inarticulate assumptions. These are more deeply rooted than abstract principles of reason; they are more stable and therefore more predictable; and they are safer and infinitely less likely to lead to violence because they leave room for compromise.

It has been said with a good deal of justice that in the first half of the nineteenth century a revolutionary situation existed in England. How was it that England not merely weathered but practically escaped the storm, and gradually readjusted her society to the new situation, whereas France was convulsed by revolution after revolution? In part, no doubt, it was because the safety valves — in pulpit, press, petition, and public meeting — were left open in England, and because the Rule of Law, in spite of many declamatory Radical protests, really did give men a conviction that things were not arbitrary, that they knew where they stood. These conditions were unlikely to give rise to that type of Messianic revolutionary experience, in which the past is viewed as completely dominated by the forces of evil, and the future — which will come after a violent break — as guaranteeing a world of harmonious perfection. Neither were such conditions likely to engender the sort of mood that makes the revolutionary trustees of posterity feel that they owe no obedience to the law of the land — which they look upon as an instrument of class exploitation and absolutist rule — but only to some unwritten law of the revolutionary Utopian future.

The truth is that the thing was psychologically impossible in England. Indeed, it is amusing to read how, during the Chartist troubles in this country, some Chartists would sigh, "Oh! we are a slovenly, slow-witted people. If we could hire some fifty professional revolutionaries from France, the thing would work!" You may remember, too, how after the Chartist failure a decision was arrived at to try physical force; but then they decided to address a request to the various branches asking them to debate the point whether to use violence or not to use violence. Legality has entered into the English subconsciousness, into the English blood. It is quite hopeless to rely on the English to make a real revolution.

As I have tried to convey, a revolution does not in modern times signify merely an uprising of protest; it means a sustained and violent effort to make all things new. I believe one is entitled to draw the conclusion from the history of the last one hundred and fifty years or so that, although Utopianism preaches peace and harmony, the sort of social revolution its pursuit involves has not proved feasible without war. Complete social transformation is impossible without totalitarianism, and this is itself impossible to sustain in an atmosphere of everyday existence. Only in an atmosphere charged with peril, with emergency actual or latent, can all opponents be branded as traitors·and the State's power over persons and property be total. The French Revolution established its hold in conditions of war; the Russian Revolution was a by-product of war; the Chinese Revolution was the result of war. The 1848 Revolutions, on the other hand, failed because there was no war.

This leads me to consider the problems facing us in the world today in the struggle between the Soviet Union, representing revolutionary Utopianism, and the West. The essence of modern Utopianism is that, to be effective, it requires universality. It claims to offer a doctrine applicable to all nations and all races. It proceeds on the assumption that it cannot permanently thrive in any one country so long as it does not thrive in all. It is in a continuous state of siege against its enemies, real or imagined, from within or from outside. It assumes, as you may read in the homely sayings of Mr. Khrushchev, that what it regards as the *Civitas Dei* must inevitably replace what it regards as the *Civitas Diaboli,* and it is quite ready to give a helping hand to the predetermined process of history.

Now, it makes all the difference in the world whether Utopians in different countries constitute, as in the nineteenth century, a

closely connected international confraternity, or whether they constitute, as in the last thirty or forty years, a single army with its
G.H.Q. in the capital of a great Power. This is so for two reasons.
First, because if the G.H.Q. is in the capital of a great Power,
then the national interests of that Power and the ideological needs
of the revolution become inseparable, and one never knows which
is which. Second, if all the Utopians act upon the assumption that
they are an army, then "their's not to reason why" or to question
the global strategy of the General Staff: they must blindly accept
and fulfill orders from G.H.Q., however disconcerting, however in-
comprehensible, however wrong.

Indeed, it has hitherto been assumed by Communists that the
Soviet system was proceeding on the lines of a deterministic science.
It was held to be foolproof. Again and again when you pointed out
to them errors or inconsistencies, they would smile at you with a
maddening superiority; they were profoundly and complacently convinced that there was a science that they alone had grasped — the
science of Marxism.

Two new factors have now been thrown into the situation. The
first is the self-questioning that has followed "de-Stalinization"; for,
if it is admitted that the régime could have been so violated, so dis-
torted, by the arbitrary action and capricious behavior of a single
tyrant, what becomes of its "scientific" character? The second factor
is the emergence of "national Communism," of the doctrine of "many
roads to Socialism," in China, in Yugoslavia, and now in Poland;
for once this doctrine is admitted, what is left of the universalism
of the ideology, the monolithic character of the movement, the un-
questioned and unquestionable infallibility of the G.H.Q.? All this
may add up to a decisive breach in the fortress. It has not happened
yet, because a fierce rearguard action is being fought; but may
we not be witnessing a decline of revolutionary Utopianism, similar
to the lowering of atmosphere that came at the end of the wars of
religion when utterly exhausted both sides realized that continued
war meant universal doom? Then "enthusiasm" became a word of
opprobrium, and men turned their attention to science and the art
of living.

Let me conclude on a different note. I believe that, potent though the craving for innovation may be at any given moment, ultimately the conservative instinct is the stronger. I believe, too, that a curse is besetting Utopianism. While it has its birth in the noblest impulses of man, it is doomed to be perverted into an instrument of tyranny and hypocrisy. For those two deep-seated urges of man, the love of freedom and the yearning for salvation, cannot be fulfilled both at the same time. But I would utter one word of warning to those who might react against Utopianism so strongly as to adopt a contemptuous, sneering attitude to human beings, to say that they are such a rotten lot that they do not deserve anything to be done for them, and to deny the possibility of constructive change and genuine progress, such as England has known from the Reform Bill to the Welfare State. Such an attitude of pessimism is unwarranted, and lacks generosity and foresight. We must try to do good — but with a full and mature knowledge of the limitations of Politics. Bertrand Russell once told us, in another context, that we had to proceed in the spirit of unyielding despair; and Georges Duhamel, the famous French writer, has said: "Toutes choses sont à leur place dans ce monde misérable, même les désirs pathétiques pour un monde meilleur."

7. Out of Utopia: Toward a Reorientation of Sociological Analysis

Ralf Dahrendorf

Then I may now proceed to tell you how I feel about the society we have just described. My feelings are much like those of a man who has beheld superb animals in a drawing, or, it may be, in real life, but at rest, and finds himself longing to behold them in motion, executing some feat commensurate with their physique. That is just how I feel about the city we have described. — Socrates in Plato's *Timaios*.

I

All utopias from Plato's Republic to George Orwell's brave new world of 1984 have had one element of construction in common: they are all societies from which change is absent. Whether conceived as a final state and climax of historical development, as an intellectual's nightmare, or as a romantic dream, the social fabric

From *The American Journal of Sociology*, vol. 64, no. 2 (September 1958), pp. 115-127.

of utopias does not, and perhaps cannot, recognize the unending flow of the historical process.[1] For the sociologist it would be an intellectual experiment both rewarding and entertaining to try and trace in, say, the totalitarian universe of 1984 potential sources of conflict and change and to predict the directions of change indicated in Big Brother's society. Its originator, of course, did not do this: his utopia would not make sense unless it was more than a passing phase of social development.

It is no accident that the catchwords of Huxley's Brave New World — "Community, Identity, Stability" — could be applied with equal justice to most other utopian constructions. Utopian societies have (to use a term popular in contemporary sociological analysis) certain structural requisites; they must display certain features in order to be what they purport to be. First, utopias do not grow out of familiar reality following realistic patterns of development. For most authors, utopias have but a nebulous past and no future; they are suddenly there, and there to stay, suspended in mid-time or, rather, somewhere beyond the ordinary notions of time. Our own society is, for the citizens of 1984, hardly more than a fading memory. Moreover, there is an unexplained gap, a kind of mutation somewhere between 1948 and 1984, interpreted in the light of arbitrary and permanently adapted "documents" prepared by the Ministry of Truth. The case of Marx is even more pertinent. It is well known how much time and energy Lenin spent in trying to link the realistically possible event of the proletarian revolution with the image of a Communist society in which there are no classes, no conflicts, no state, and, indeed, no division of labor. Lenin, as we know, failed, in theory as in practice, to get beyond the "dictatorship of the proletariat," and somehow we are not surprised at that. It is hard to link, by rational argument or empirical analysis, the wide river of history — flowing more rapidly at some points, more slowly at others, but always moving — and the tranquil village pond of utopia.

Nor are we surprised that in social reality the "dictatorship of the proletariat" soon turned out to be more and more of the former, involving less and less of the latter.

A second structural characteristic of utopias seems to be the uniformity of such societies or, to use more technical language, the existence of universal consensus on prevailing values and institutional arrangements. This, too, will prove relevant for the explanation of the impressive stability of all utopias. Consensus on values and institutions does not necessarily mean that utopias cannot in some ways be democratic. Consensus can be enforced — as it is for Orwell — or it can be spontaneous, a kind of *contrat social* — as it is for some eighteenth-century utopian writers, and, if in a perverted way, i.e., by conditioned spontaneity, again for Huxley. One might suspect, on closer inspection, that, from the point of view of political organization, the result would in both cases turn out to be rather similar. But this line of analysis involves critical interpretation and will be postponed for the moment. Suffice it to note that the assumption of universal consensus seems to be built into most utopian constructions and is apparently one of the factors explaining their stability.

Universal consensus means, by implication, absence of structurally generated conflict. In fact, many builders of utopias go to considerable lengths to convince their audience that in their societies conflict about values or institutional arrangements is either impossible or simply unnecessary. Utopias are perfect — be it perfectly agreeable or perfectly disagreeable — and consequently there is nothing to quarrel about. Strikes and revolutions are as conspicuously absent from utopian societies as are parliaments in which organized groups advance their conflicting claims for power. Utopian societies may be and, indeed, often are caste societies; but they are not class societies in which the oppressed revolt against their oppressors. We may note, third, that social harmony seems to be one of the factors adduced to account for utopian stability.[2]

Some writers add to their constructions a particularly clever touch of realism: they invent an individual who does not conform to the accepted values and ways of life. Orwell's Winston Smith or Huxley's Savage are cases in point — but it is not difficult to imagine a surviving capitalist in Communist society or similar villains of the peace in other utopias. For exigencies of this kind, utopias usually have varied, though effective, means at their disposal to do away with the disturbers of unity. But how did they emerge in the first place? That question is rather more difficult to answer. Characteristically, utopian writers take refuge in chance to carry off this paradox. Their "outsiders" are not (and cannot be) products of the social structure of utopia but deviants, pathological cases infected with some unique disease.

In order to make their constructions at all realistic, utopians must, of course, allow for some activities and processes in their society. The difference between utopia and a cemetery is that occasionally some things do happen in utopia. But — and this is the fourth point — all processes going on in utopian societies follow recurrent patterns and occur within, and as part of, the design of the whole. Not only do they not upset the status quo: they affirm and sustain it, and it is in order to do so that most utopians allow them to happen at all. For example, most writers have retained the idea that men are mortal, even in utopia.[3] Some provisions, therefore, have to be made for the reproduction, both physical and social, of society. Sexual intercourse (or at least artificial fertilization), the upbringing and education of children, and selection for social positions have to be secured and regulated — to mention only the minimum of social institutions required simply because men are mortal.[4] In addition to this, most utopian constructions have to cope in some way with the division of labor. These regulated processes are, however, no more than the metabolism of society; they are part and parcel of the general consensus on values, and they serve to uphold the existing state of affairs. Although some of its parts are moving in predetermined, calculable ways, utopia as a whole remains a *perpetuum immobile*.

Finally, to add a more obvious observation, utopias generally seem to be curiously isolated from all other communities (if such are indeed assumed to exist at all). We have already mentioned isolation in time, but usually we also find isolation in space. Citizens of utopia are seldom allowed to travel, and, if they are, their reports will serve to magnify, rather than bridge, the differences between utopia and the rest of the world. Utopias are monolithic and homogeneous communities, suspended not only in time but also in space, shut off from the outside world, which might, after all, present a threat to the cherished immobility of the social structure.

There are other features which most utopian constructions have in common, and which it might be interesting for the sociologist to investigate. Also, the question might be asked, Just how pleasant would it be to live in even the most benevolent of utopias? Karl Popper, in his *Open Society and Its Enemies,* has explored these and other aspects of closed and utopian societies at considerable detail, and there is little to add to his incisive analyses.[5] Our concern is of a rather more specific nature than the investigation of some common structural elements of utopia. We now propose to ask the seemingly pointless, and even naive, question whether we actually encounter all or any of these elements in *real* societies.

One of the advantages of the naiveté of this question is that it is easily answered. A society without history? There are, of course, "new societies" like the United States in the seventeenth and eighteenth centuries; there are "primitive societies" in a period of transition from preliterate to literate culture. But in either case it would be not only misleading but downright false to say that there are no antecedents, no historical roots, no developmental patterns linking these societies with the past. A society with universal consensus? One without conflict? We know that without the assistance of a secret police it has never been possible to produce such a state and that even the threat of police persecution can, at best, prevent dissensus and conflict from finding expression in open struggles for limited periods of time. A society isolated in space and devoid of processes upsetting or changing its design? Anthropologists have occasionally asserted that such societies do exist, but it has never taken very long to disprove their assertions. In fact, there is no need to discuss these questions very seriously. It is obvious that such societies do not exist — just as it is obvious that every known society changes its values and institutions continuously. Changes may be rapid or gradual, violent or regulated, comprehensive or piecemeal, but it is never entirely absent where human beings create organizations to live together.

These are commonplaces about which even sociologists will hardly disagree. In any case, utopia means Nowhere, and the very construction of a utopian society implies that it has no equivalent in reality. The writer building his world in Nowhere has the advantage of being able to ignore the commonplaces of the real world. He can populate the moon, telephone to Mars, let flowers speak and horses fly, he can even make history come to a standstill — so long as he does not confound his imagination with reality, in which case he is doomed to the fate of Plato in Syracuse, Owen in Harmony, Lenin in Russia.

Obvious as these observations may be, it is at this point that the question arises which explains our interest in the social structure of utopia and which appears to merit some more detailed examination: If the immobility of utopia, its isolation in time and space, the absence of conflict and disruptive processes, is a product of poetic imagination divorced from the commonplaces of reality — how is it that so much of recent sociological theory has been based on exactly these assumptions and has, in fact, consistently operated with a utopian model of society?[6] What are the reasons and what the consequences of the fact that every one of the elements we found characteristic of the social structure of utopia reappears in the attempt to systematize our knowledge of society and formulate sociological propositions of a generalizing nature?

It would evidently be both misleading and unfair to impute to any sociologist the explicit intention to view society as an unmoving entity of eternal stability. In fact, the commonplace that wherever there is social life there is change can be found at the outset of most sociological treatises. I contend, however, in this paper that (1) recent theoretical approaches, by analyzing social structure in terms of the elements characteristic of immobile societies, have, in fact, assumed the utopian image of society; that (2) this assumption, particularly if associated with the claim to being the most general, or even the only possible, model, has been detrimental to the advancement of sociological research; and that (3) it has to be replaced by a more useful and realistic approach to the analysis of social structure and social process.

II

Much of the theoretical discussion in contemporary sociology reminds me of a Platonic dialogue. Both share an atmosphere of unrealism, lack of controversy, and irrelevance. To be sure, I am not suggesting that there is or has been a Socrates in our profession. But, as with Plato's dialogues, somebody selects for essentially arbitrary reasons a topic or, more often, a general area of inquiry and, at the same time, states his position. Then there is some initial disagreement. Gradually disagreement gives way to an applauding, but disengaged and unconvincing, murmur of "Indeed," or "You don't say." Then the topic is forgotten — it has nothing to do with anything in particular anyway — and we move on to another one, starting the game all over again (or else we turn away in disgust from the enterprise of theory altogether). In this process, Plato at least managed to convey to us a moral and metaphysical view of the world; we, the scientists, have not even been able to do that.

I am reminded of Plato in yet a more specific sense. There is a curious similarity between the *Republic* — at least from the second book onward[7] — and a certain line of sociological reasoning rather prominent in these days and by no means associated with only one or two names. In the *Republic,* Socrates and his partners set out to explore the meaning of δικανοσύγη , "justice." In modern sociological theory we have set out to explore the meaning of "equilibrium" or, as it is sometimes called, "homeostasis." Socrates soon finds out that justice really means το ἑαυτοῦ πράττεγγ, that everybody does what is incumbent upon him. We have discovered that equilibrium means that everybody plays his role. To illustrate this, Socrates and his friends go about the business of constructing a theoretical — and presumably ideal — πόλιϛ. We have constructed the "social system." In the end, both Plato and we are left with a perfect society which has a structure, is functioning, is in equilibrium, and is therefore just. However, what are we going to do with it? With his blueprint in mind, Plato went to the assistance of his friend Dion in Syracuse and tried to realize it. He failed miserably. Plato was wise, he admitted defeat. Without abandoning his idea of the best of all possible worlds, he decided that perhaps, so far as real human beings and real circumstances were concerned, democracy with all its shortcomings was a more effective way to proceed.[8] We have not yet been quite as wise. Although what we still tend to call "theory" has failed as miserably in tackling real problems as Plato's blueprint, we have so far not admitted defeat.

The social system, like utopia, has not grown out of familiar reality. Instead of abstracting a limited number of variables and postulating their relevance for the explanation of a particular problem, it represents a huge and allegedly all-embracing superstructure of concepts that do not describe, propositions that do not explain, and models from which nothing follows. At least they do not describe or explain (or underlie explanations of) the real world with which we are concerned. For much of our theorizing about social systems the same objection holds that Milton Friedman raised against Lange's "Economic System":

> [He] largely dispenses with the initial step of theory — a full and comprehensive set of observed and related facts to be generalized — and in the main reaches conclusions no observed facts can contradict. His emphasis is on the formal structure of the theory, the logical interrelations of the parts. He considers it largely unnecessary to test the validity of his theoretical structure except for conformity to the canons of formal logic. His categories are selected primarily to facilitate logical analysis, not empirical application or test. For the most part, the crucial question, "What observed facts would contradict the generalization suggested and what operations could be followed to observe such critical facts?" is never asked; and the theory is so set up that it could seldom be answered if it were asked. The theory provides formal models of imaginary worlds, not generalizations about the real world.[9]

Consensus on values is one of the prime features of the social system. Some of its advocates make a slight concession to reality and speak of "relative consensus," thereby indicating their contempt for both the canons of scientific theory (in the models of which there is no place for "relatives" or "almosts") and the observable facts of reality (which show little evidence of any more than highly formal — and tautological — consensus). That societies are held together by some kind of value consensus seems to me either a definition of societies or a statement clearly contradicted by empirical evidence — unless one is concerned not so much with real societies and their problems as with social systems in which anything might be true, including the integration of all socially held values into a religious doctrine. I have yet to see a problem for the explanation of which the assumption of a unified value system is necessary, or a testable prediction that follows from this assumption.

It is hard to see how a social system based on ("almost") universal consensus can allow for structurally generated conflicts. Presumably, conflict always implies some kind of dissensus and disagreement about values. In Christian theology original sin was required to explain the transition from paradise to history. Private property has been no less a *deus ex machina* in Marx's attempt to account for the transition from an early society, in which "man felt as much at home as a fish in the water," to a world of alienation and class struggles.[10] Both these explanations may not be very satisfactory; they at least permit recognition of the hard and perhaps unpleasant facts of real life. Modern sociological theory of the structural-functional variety has failed to do even that (unless one wants to regard the curiously out-of-place chapter on change in Talcott Parsons' *Social System* as the original sin of this approach). By no feat of the imagination, not even by the residual category of "dysfunction," can the integrated and equilibrated social system be made to produce serious and patterned conflicts in its structure.

What the social system can produce, however, is the well-known villain of the peace of utopia, the "deviant." Even he requires some considerable argument and the introduction of a chance, or at least an undetermined variable — in this case, individual psychology. Although the system is perfect and in a state of equilibrium, individuals cannot always live up to this perfection. "Deviance is a motivated tendency for an actor to behave in contravention of one or more institutionalized normative patterns" (Parsons).[11] Motivated by what, though? Deviance occurs either if an individual happens to be pathological, or, if, *"from whatever source* [this, of course, being unspecified], a disturbance is introduced into the system."[12] In other words, it occurs for sociologically — and that means structurally — unknown and unknowable reasons. It is the bacillus that befalls the system from the dark depths of the individual psyche or the nebulous reaches of the outside world. Fortunately, the system has at its disposal certain mechanisms to deal with the deviant and to "re-equilibrate" itself, i.e., the mechanisms of social control.

The striking preoccupation of sociological theory with the related problems of reproduction, socialization, and role allocation or, on the institutional level, with (in this sequence) the family, the educational system, and the division of labor fits in well with our comparison of this type of theory and utopian societies. Plato carefully avoided Justinian's static definition of justice as *suum cuique;* in his definition the emphasis is on πράττειν, on the active and, to apply a much abused term, dynamic aspect. Similarly, the structural-functionalist insists on his concern not with a static but with a moving equilibrium. But what does this moving equilibrium mean? It means, in the last analysis, that the system is a structure not of the building type but of the organism type. Homeostasis is maintained by the regular occurrence of certain patterned processes which, far from disturbing the tranquillity of the village pond, in fact *are* the village pond. Heraclitus' saying, "We enter the same river, and it is not the same," does not hold here. The system is the same, however often we look at it. Children are born and socialized and allocated until they die; new children are born, and the same happens all over again. What a peaceful, what an idyllic, world the system is! Of course, it is not static in the sense of being dead; things happen all the time; but — alas! — they are under control, and they all help to maintain that precious equilibrium of the whole. Things not only happen, but they function, and so long as that is the case, all is well.

One of the more unfortunate connotations of the word "system" is its closure. Although some structural-functionalists have tried, there is no getting away from the fact that a system is essentially something that is — even if only "for purposes of analysis" —

self-sufficient, internally consistent, and closed to the outside. A leg cannot be called a system; a body can. Actually, advocates of the system have little reason to be unhappy with this term; abandoning it would rob their analyses of much of their neatness and, above all, would disable them with respect to the "whatever sources" — the villainous outsiders they can now introduce to "account" for unwanted realities. I do not want to go too far in my polemics, but I cannot help feeling that it is only a step from thinking about societies in terms of equilibrated systems to asserting that every disturber of the equilibrium, every deviant, is a "spy" or an "imperialistic agent." The system theory of society comes, by implication, dangerously close to the conspiracy-theory of history — which is not only the end of all sociology but also rather silly.[13] There is nothing logically wrong with the term "system." It begins to give birth to all kinds of undesirable consequences only when it is applied to total societies and is made the ultimate frame of reference of analysis. It is certainly true that sociology deals with society. But it is equally true that physics deals with nature, and yet physicists would hardly see an advance in calling nature a system and trying to analyze it as such. In fact, the attempt to do so would probably — and justly — be discarded as metaphysics.

To repeat, the social system as conceived by some recent sociological theorists appears to be characterized by the same features as those contained in utopian societies. This being so, the conclusion is forced upon us that this type of theory also deals with societies from which historical change is absent and that it is, in this sense, utopian. To be sure, it is utopian not because some of the assumptions of this theory are "unrealistic" — this would be true for the assumptions of almost any scientific theory — but because it is exclusively concerned with spelling out the conditions of the functioning of a utopian social system. Structural-functional theory does not introduce unrealistic assumptions for the purpose of explaining real problems; it introduces many kinds of assumptions, concepts, and models for the sole purpose of describing a social system that has never existed and is not likely ever to come into being.

In thus comparing the social system with utopia, I feel I have done an injustice to the majority of utopian writers which needs to be corrected. With few exceptions, the purpose underlying utopian constructions has been one of criticism, even indictment, of existing societies. The story of utopias is the story of an intensely moral and polemical branch of human thinking and, although, from a realistic and political point of view, utopian writers may have chosen doubtful means to express their values, they have certainly succeeded in conveying to their times a strong concern with the shortcomings and injustices of existing institutions and beliefs. This can hardly be said of modern sociological theory. The sense of complacency with — if not justification of — the status quo, which, by intention or default, pervades the structural-functional school of social thought is unheard of in utopian literature. Even as utopias go, the social system is rather a weak link in a tradition of penetrating and often radical criticism. I do not want to suggest that sociology should be primarily concerned with uncovering and indicting the evils of society; but I do want to assert that those sociologists who felt that they had to embark on a utopian venture were rather ill-advised in retaining the technical imperfections while at the same time abandoning the moral impulses of their numerous forerunners.

III

It is easy to be polemical, hard to be constructive, and — at least for me — impossible to be as impressively and happily catholic as those at whom my critical comments are directed. However, I do not propose to evade the just demand to specify whose work I mean when I refer to the utopian nature of sociological theory, to explain why I think that an approach of this kind is useless and even detrimental for our discipline, and to describe what better ways there are in my opinion to deal with our problems.

The name that comes to mind immediately when one speaks about sociological theory in these days is that of Talcott Parsons. Already, in many discussions and for many people, Parsons appears to be more of a symbol than a reality. Let me therefore state quite explicitly that my criticism applies neither to Parsons' total work nor only to his work. I am not concerned with Parsons' excellent and important philosophical analysis of *The Structure of Social Action,* nor am I concerned with his numerous perceptive contributions to the understanding of empirical phenomena. I do think, however, that much of his theoretical work in the last ten years represents an outstanding illustration of what I mean by the utopian bent in sociological theory. The double emphasis on the articulation of purely formal conceptual frameworks and on the social system as the point of departure and arrival of sociological analysis involves all the vices and, in his case, none of the virtues of a utopian approach. But, in stating this, one should not overlook that at some time or other many prominent American sociologists and some British anthropologists have engaged in the same kind of reasoning.

Two main remedies have been proposed in recent years against the malady of utopianism. In my opinion they have both been based on a wrong diagnosis — and by correcting this diagnostic error we may hope to get to the root of the trouble and at the same time to a path that promises to lead us out of utopia.

For some time now it has been quite popular in our profession to support T. H. Marshall's demand for "sociological stepping stones in the middle distance" or Robert K. Merton's plea for "theories of the middle range." I cannot say that I am very happy with these formulations. True, both Marshall and Merton explain at some length what they mean by their formulas. In particular, they advocate something they call a "convergence" of theory and research. But "convergence" is a very mechanical notion of a process that defies the laws of mechanics. Above all, this conception implies that sociological theory and sociological research are two separate activities which it is possible to divide and to join. I do not believe that this is so. In fact, I think that, so long as we hold this belief, our theory will be logical and philosophical, and our research will at best be sociographic, with sociology disappearing in the gorge between these two. The admonitions of Marshall and Merton may

actually have led to a commendable rediscovery of empirical problems of investigation, but I venture to assert that, looking purely at
their formulations, this has been an unintended consequence, a by-
product rather than the content of their statements.[14]

There is no theory that can be divorced from empirical research;
but, of course, the reverse is equally true. I have no sympathy with
the confusion of the just demand that sociological analysis should
be inspired by empirical problems and the unjust demand that it
should be based on or even exclusively concerned with something
called "empirical research." As a matter of fact, the advocates of
"empirical research" and the defenders of abstract theory have been
strikingly similar in one, to my mind crucial, respect (which explains, by the way, why they have been able to coexist with com-
paratively little friction and controversy): they have both largely
dispensed with that prime impulse of all science and scholarship,
with the puzzlement over specific, concrete, and — if this word must
be used — empirical problems. Many sociologists have lost the
simple impulse of curiosity, the desire to solve riddles of experience,
the concern with problems. This, rather than anything else, explains
both the success and the danger of the utopian fallacy in sociological
thinking and of its smaller brother, the fallacy of empirical research.

It is perhaps fairly obvious that a book like *The Social System*
displays but a minimal concern with riddles of experience. But I do
not want to be misunderstood. My plea for a reinstatement of empirical problems in the central place that is due to them is by no
means merely a plea for greater recognition of "facts," "data," or
"empirical evidence." I think that, from the point of view of concern
with problems, there is very little to choose between *The Social System* and the ever increasing number of undoubtedly well-documented
Ph.D. theses on such subjects as "The Social Structure of a Hospi-
tal," "The Role of the Professional Football Player," and "Family
Relations in a New York Suburb." "Areas of Investigation," "Fields
of Inquiry," "Subjects," and "Topics," chosen because nobody has
studied them before or for some other random reason, are not problems. What I mean is that at the outset of every scientific investigation there has to be a fact or set of facts that is puzzling the in-

vestigator; children of businessmen prefer professional to business occupations; workers in the automobile industry of Detroit go on strike; there is a higher incidence of suicides among upwardly mobile persons than among others; Socialist parties in predominantly Catholic countries of Europe seem unable to get more than 30 per cent of the popular vote; Hungarian people revolt against the Communist regime. There is no need to enumerate more of such facts; what matters is that every one of them invites the question "Why?" and it is this question, after all, which has always inspired that noble human activity in which we are engaged — science.

There is little point in restating methodological platitudes. Let me confine myself, therefore, to saying that a scientific discipline that is problem-conscious at every stage of its development is very unlikely ever to find itself in the prison of utopian thought or to separate theory and research. Problems require explanation; explanations require assumptions or models and hypotheses derived from such models; hypotheses, which are always, by implication, predictions as well as explanatory propositions, require testing by further facts; testing often generates new problems.[15] If anybody wants to distinguish theory and research in this process, he is welcome to do so; my own feeling is that this distinction confuses, rather than clarifies, our thinking.

The loss of problem-consciousness in modern sociology explains many of the drawbacks of the present state of our discipline and, in particular, the utopian character of sociological theory; moreover, it is in itself a problem worthy of investigation. How was it that sociologists, of all people, could lose touch with the riddles of experience, of which there are so many in the social world? At this point, I think, the ideological interpretation of sociological development which has recently been advanced by a number of authors is pertinent.[16] By turning away from the critical facts of experience, sociologists have both followed and strengthened the trend toward conservatism that is so powerful in the intellectual world today. What is more, their conservatism is not of the militant kind found in the so-called Left Wing of the conservative parties in England, France, Germany, and the U.S.; it is, rather, a conservatism by implication, the conservatism of complacency. I am sure that Parsons and many of those who have joined him in utopia would disclaim being conservatives, and, so far as their explicit political convictions go, there is no reason to doubt their sincerity. At the same time, their way of looking at society or, rather, of not looking at society when they should, has promoted a sense of disengagement, of not wanting to worry about things, and has, in fact, elevated this attitude of abstinence to a "scientific theory" according to which there is no need to worry. By thus leaving the job of worrying to the powers that be, sociologists have implicitly recognized the legitimacy of these powers; their disengagement has turned out to be a — however involuntary — engagement on the side of the status quo. What a dramatic misunderstanding of Max Weber's attempt to separate the vocation of politics from that of science!

Let me repeat that I am not advocating a sociological science that is politically radical in the content of its theories. In any case, there would be little sense in trying to do this, since, logically speaking, there can be no such science. I am advocating however, a sociological science that is inspired by the moral fiber of its forefathers; and I am convinced that if we regain the problem-consciousness which has been lost in the last decades, we cannot fail to recover the critical engagement in the realities of our social world which we need to do our job well. For I hope I have made it quite clear that problem-consciousness is not merely a means of avoiding ideological biases but is, above all, an indispensable condition of progress in any discipline of human inquiry. The path out of utopia begins with the recognition of puzzling facts of experience and the tackling of problems posed by such facts.

There is yet another reason why I think the utopian character of recent sociological theory has been detrimental to the advancement of our discipline. It is quite conceivable that in the explanation of specific problems we shall at some stage want to employ models of a highly general kind or even formulate general laws. Stripped of its more formal and decorative elements, the social system could be — and sometimes has been — regarded as such a model. For instance, we may want to investigate the problem of why achievement in the educational system ranks so high among people's concerns in our society. The social system can be thought of as suggesting that in advanced industrial societies the educational system is the main, and tends to be the only, mechanism of role allocation. In this case, the social system proves to be a useful model. It seems to me, however, that even in this limited sense the social system is a highly problematic, or at least a very one-sided, model and that here, too, a new departure is needed.

It is perhaps inevitable that the models underlying scientific explanations acquire a life of their own, divorced from the specific purpose for which they have originally been constructed. The *Homo economicus* of modern economics, invented in the first place as a useful, even if clearly unrealistic, assumption from which testable hypotheses could be derived, has today become the cardinal figure in a much discussed philosophy of human nature far beyond the aspirations of most economists. The indeterminacy principle in modern physics, which again is nothing but a useful assumption without claim to any reality other than operational, has been taken as a final refutation of all determinist philosophies of nature. Analogous statements could be made about the equilibrium model of society — although, as I have tried to show, it would unfortunately be wrong to say that the original purpose of this model was to explain specific empirical problems. We face the double task of having to specify the conditions under which this model proves analytically useful and of having to cope with the philosophical implications of the model itself.[17] It may seem a digression for a sociologist to occupy himself with the latter problem; however, in my opinion it is both dangerous and irresponsible to ignore the implications of one's assumptions, even if these are philosophical rather than scientific in a technical sense. The models with which we work, apart from being useful tools, determine to no small extent our general perspectives, our selection of problems, and the emphasis in our explanations, and I believe that in this respect, too, the utopian social system has played an unfortunate role in our discipline.

There may be some problems for the explanation of which it is important to assume an equilibrated, functioning social system based on consensus, absence of conflict, and isolation in time and space. I think there are such problems, although their number is probably much smaller than many contemporary sociologists wish us to believe. The equilibrium model of society also has a long tradition in social thinking, including, of course, all utopian thinking but also such works as Rousseau's *Contrat social* and Hegel's *Philosophy of Law*. But neither in relation to the explanation of sociological problems nor in the history of social philosophy is it the only model, and I would strongly protest any implicit or explicit claim that it can be so regarded. Parsons' statement in *The Social System* that this "work constitutes a step toward the development of a generalized theoretical system"[18] is erroneous in every respect I can think of and, in particular, insofar as it implies that all sociological problems can be approached with the equilibrium model of society.

It may be my personal bias that I can think of many more problems to which the social system does not apply than those to which it does, but I would certainly insist that, even on the highly abstract and largely philosophical level on which Parsons moves, at least one other model of society is required. It has an equally long and, I think, a better tradition than the equilibrium model. In spite of this fact, no modern sociologist has as yet formulated its basic tenets in such a way as to render it useful for the explanation of critical social facts. Only in the last year or two has there been some indication that this alternative model, which I shall call the "conflict model of society," is gaining ground in sociological analysis.

The extent to which the social system model has influenced even our thinking about social change and has marred our vision in this important area of problems is truly remarkable. Two facts in particular illustrate this influence. In talking about change, most sociologists today accept the entirely spurious distinction between "change within" and "change of societies," which makes sense only if we recognize the system as our ultimate and only reference point. At the same time, many sociologists seem convinced that, in order to explain processes of change, they have to discover certain special circumstances which set these processes in motion, implying that, in society, change is an abnormal, or at least an unusual, state that has to be accounted for in terms of deviations from a "normal," equilibrated system. I think that in both these respects we shall have to revise our assumptions radically. A Galilean turn of thought is required which makes us realize that all units of social organization are continuously changing, unless some force intervenes to arrest this change. It is our task to identify the factors interfering with the normal process of change rather than to look for variables involved in bringing about change. Moreover, change is ubiquitous not only in time but also in space, that is to say, every part of societies is constantly changing, and it is impossible to distinguish between "change within" and "change of," "microscopic" and "macroscopic" change. Historians discovered a long time ago that in describing the historical process it is insufficient to confine one's attention to the affairs of state, to wars, revolutions, and government action. From them we could learn that what happens in Mrs. Smith's house, in a trade union local, or in the parish of a church is just as significant for the social process of history and, in fact, *is* just as much the social process of history as what happens in the White House or the Kremlin.

The great creative force that carries along change in the model I am trying to describe and that is equally ubiquitous is social conflict. The notion that wherever there is social life there is conflict may be unpleasant and disturbing. Nevertheless, it is indispensable to our understanding of social problems. As with change, we have grown accustomed to look for special causes or circumstances whenever we encounter conflict; but, again, a complete turn is necessary in our thinking. Not the presence but the absence of conflict is surprising and abnormal, and we have good reason to be suspicious if we find a society or social organization that displays no evidence of conflict. To be sure, we do not have to assume that conflict is always violent and uncontrolled. There is probably a continuum from civil war to parliamentary debate, from strikes and lockouts to joint consultation. Our problems and their explanations will undoubtedly teach us a great deal about the range of variation in forms of conflict. In formulating such explanations, however, we must never lose sight of the underlying assumption that conflict can be temporarily suppressed, regulated, channeled, and controlled but that neither a philosopher-king nor a modern dictator can abolish it once and for all.

There is a third notion which, together with change and conflict, constitutes the instrumentarium of the conflict model of society: the notion of constraint. From the point of view of this model, societies and social organizations are held together not by consensus but by constraint, not by universal agreement but by the coercion of some by others. It may be useful for some purposes to speak of the "value system" of a society, but in the conflict model such characteristic values are ruling rather than common, enforced rather than accepted, at any given point of time. And as conflict generates change, so constraint may be thought of as generating conflict. We assume that conflict is ubiquitous, since constraint is ubiquitous wherever human beings set up social organizations. In a highly formal sense, it is always the basis of constraint that is at issue in social conflict.

I have sketched the conflict model of society — as I see it — only very briefly. But except in a philosophical context there is no need to elaborate on it, unless, of course, such elaboration is required for the explanation of specific problems. However, my point here is a different one. I hope it is evident that there is a fundamental difference between the equilibrium and the conflict models of society. Utopia is — to use the language of the economist — a world of certainty. It is paradise found; utopians know all the answers. But we live in a world of uncertainty. We do not know what an ideal society looks like — and if we think we do, we are fortunately unable to realize our conception. Because there is no certainty (which, by definition, is shared by everybody in that condition), there has to be constraint to assure some livable minimum of coherence. Because we do not know all the answers, there has to be continuous conflict over values and policies. Because of uncertainty, there is always change and development. Quite apart from its merits as a tool of scientific analysis, the conflict model is essentially non-utopian; it is the model of an open society.

I do not intend to fall victim to the mistake of many structural-functional theorists and advance for the conflict model a claim to comprehensive and exclusive applicability. As far as I can see, we need for the explanation of sociological problems both the equilibrium and the conflict models of society; and it may well be that, in a philosophical sense, society has two faces of equal reality: one of stability, harmony, and consensus and one of change, conflict, and constraint.[19] Strictly speaking, it does not matter whether we select for investigation problems that can be understood only in terms of the equilibrium model or problems for the explanation of which the conflict model is required. There is no intrinsic criterion for preferring one to the other. My own feeling is, however, that, in the face of recent developments in our discipline and the critical considerations offered earlier in this paper, we may be well advised to concentrate in the future not only on concrete problems but on such problems as involve explanations in terms of constraint, conflict, and change. This second face of society may aesthetically be rather less pleasing than the social system — but, if all that sociology had to offer were an easy escape to utopian tranquillity, it would hardly be worth our efforts.

NOTES

1. There are very many utopian constructions, particularly in recent decades. Since these vary considerably, it is doubtful whether any generalization can apply to all of them. I have tried to be careful in my generalizations on this account and to generalize without reservation only where I feel this can be defended. Thus I am prepared to argue the initial thesis of this paper even against such assertions as H. G. Wells': "The Modern Utopia must not be static but kinetic, must shape not as a permanent state but as a hopeful stage, leading to a long ascent of stages" (*A Modern Utopia* [London: T. Nelson & Sons, 1909], chap. i, sec. 1). It seems to me that the crucial distinction to make here is that between intrasystem processes, i.e., changes that are actually part of the design of utopia, and historical change, the direction and outcome of which is not predetermined.

2. R. Gerber states, in his study of *Utopian Fantasy* (London: Routledge, 1955): "The most admirably constructed Utopia fails to convince if we are not led to believe that the danger of revolt is excluded" (p. 68).
3. Although many writers have been toying with the idea of immortality as conveyed by either divine grace or the progress of medical science. Why utopian writers should be concerned with this idea may be explained, in part, by the observations offered in this paper.
4. In fact, the subjects of sex, education, role allocation, and division of labor loom large in utopian writing from its Platonic beginnings.
5. Others authors could and should, of course, be mentioned who have dealt extensively with utopia and its way of life. Sociologically most relevant are L. Mumford, *The Story of Utopias* (New York: P. Smith, 1941); K. Mannheim, *Ideology and Utopia* (New York: Harcourt, Brace, 1936 [trans. by L. Wirth and E. Shils]; M. Buber, *Paths in Utopia* (New York: Macmillan, 1950 [trans. by R. F. C. Hull]).
6. In this essay I am concerned mainly with recent sociological theory. I have the impression, however, that much of the analysis offered here also applies to earlier works in social theory and that, in fact, the utopian model of society is one of two models which reappear throughout the history of Western philosophy. Expansion of the argument to a more general historical analysis of social thought might be a task both instructive and rewarding.
7. The first book of the *Republic* has always struck me as a remarkable exception to the general pattern of Plato's Socratic dialogues. (It is, of course, well established that this book was written considerably earlier than the rest of the *Republic*.) Whereas I have little sympathy with the content of Thrasymachus' argument in defense of the "right of the strongest," I have every sympathy with his insistence, which makes this book much more controversial and interesting than any other dialogue.
8. I am aware that this account telescopes the known facts considerably and overstresses Plato's intention to realize the Ideal State in Syracuse. The education of Dion's son was obviously a very indirect way of doing so. However, there is enough truth even in the overstatement offered here to make it a useful argument.
9. Milton Friedman, "Lange on Price Flexibility and Employment," in *Essays in Positive Economics* (Chicago: University

of Chicago Press, 1953), p. 283. The following sentences of Friedman's critique are also pertinent (pp. 283 ff.): "Lange starts with a number of abstract functions whose relevance — though not their form or content — is suggested by casual observation of the world.... He then largely leaves the real world and, in effect, seeks to enumerate all possible economic systems to which these functions could give rise.... Having completed his enumeration, or gone as far as he can or thinks desirable, Lange then seeks to relate his theoretical structure to the real world by judging to which of his alternative possibilities the real world corresponds. Is it any wonder that 'very special conditions' will have to be satisfied to explain the real world?... There are an infinite number of theoretical systems; there are only a few real worlds."

10. Marx tackled this problem in the Paris manuscripts of 1845 on *Economics and Philosophy*. This entire work is an outstanding illustration of the philosophical and analytical problems faced in any attempt to relate utopia and reality.

11. *The Social System* (New York: The Free Press, 1951), p. 250.

12. *Ibid.*, p. 252; my italics.

13. It could, for instance, be argued that only totalitarian states display one unified value system and that only in the case of totalitarian systems do we have to assume some outside influence ("from whatever source") to account for change — an argument that clearly reduces the extreme structural-functional position to absurdity.

14. Most of the works of Marshall and Merton do display the kind of concern with problems which I am here advocating. My objection to their formulations is therefore not directed against these works but against their explicit assumption that all that is wrong with recent history is its generality and that by simply reducing the level of generality we can solve all problems.

15. It is, however, essential to this approach — to add one not so trivial methodological point — that we realize the proper function of empirical testing. As Popper has demonstrated in many of his works since 1935 (the year of publication of *Logik der Forschung*), there can be no verification in science; empirical tests serve to falsify accepted theories, and every refutation of a theory is a triumph of scientific research. Testing that is designed to confirm hypotheses neither advances our knowledge nor generates new problems.

16. I am thinking in particular of the still outstanding articles by S. M. Lipset and R. Bendix on "Social Status and Social Structure," *British Journal of Sociology*, Vol. II (1951), and of the

early parts of L. Coser's work, *The Functions of Social Conflict* (New York: The Free Press, 1956).

17. The approach here characterized by the catchword "social system" has two aspects which are not necessarily related and which I am here treating separately. One is its concentration on formal "conceptual frameworks" of no relevance to particular empirical problems, as discussed in the previous section. The other aspect lies in the application of an equilibrium model of society to the analysis of real societies and is dealt with in the present section. The emphasis of advocates of the social system on one or the other of these aspects has been shifting, and to an extent it is possible to accept the one without the other. Both aspects, however, betray the traces of utopianism, and it is therefore indicated to deal with both of them in an essay that promises to show a path out of utopia.

18. Characteristically, this statement is made in the chapter "The Processes of Change of Social System" (p. 486). In many ways I have here taken this chapter of *The Social System* as a clue to problems of structural-functionalism — an approach which a page-by-page interpretation of the amazingly weak argument offered by Parsons in support of his double claim that (*a*) the stabilized system is the central point of reference of sociological analysis and (*b*) any theory of change is impossible as the present state of our knowledge could easily justify.

19. I should not be prepared to claim that these two are the only possible models of sociological analysis. Without any doubt, we need a considerable number of models on many levels for the explanation of specific problems, and, more often than not, the two models outlined here are too general to be of immediate relevance. In philosophical terms, however, it is hard to see what other models of society there could be which are not of either the equilibrium or the conflict type.

8: America in the Technetronic Age

Zbigniew Brzezinski

Ours is no longer the conventional revolutionary era; we are entering a novel metamorphic phase in human history. The world is on the eve of a transformation more dramatic in its historic and human consequences than that wrought either by the French or the Bolshevik revolutions. Viewed from a long perspective, these famous revolutions merely scratched the surface of the human condition. The changes they precipitated involved alterations in the distribution of power and property within society; they did not affect the essence of individual and social existence. Life — personal and organized — continued much as before, even though some of its external forms (primarily political) were substantially altered. Shocking though it may sound to their acolytes, by the year 2000 it will be accepted that Robespierre and Lenin were mild reformers.

Unlike the revolutions of the past, the developing metamorphosis will have no charismatic leaders with strident doctrines, but its impact will be far more profound. Most of the change that has so far taken place in human history has been gradual — with the great

From *Encounter*, vol. 30, no. 1 (January 1968), pp. 16-26.

"revolutions" being mere punctuation marks to a slow, eludible process. In contrast, the approaching transformation will come more rapidly and will have deeper consequences for the way and even perhaps for the meaning of human life than anything experienced by the generations that preceded us.

America is already beginning to experience these changes and in the course of so doing it is becoming a "technetronic" society: a society that is shaped culturally, psychologically, socially, and economically by the impact of technology and electronics, particularly computers and communications. The industrial process no longer is the principal determinant of social change, altering the mores, the social structure, and the values of society. This change is separating the United States from the rest of the world, prompting a further fragmentation among an increasingly differentiated mankind, and imposing upon Americans a special obligation to ease the pains of the resulting confrontation.

THE TECHNETRONIC SOCIETY

The far-reaching innovations we are about to experience will be the result primarily of the impact of science and technology on man and his society, especially in the developed world. Recent years have seen a proliferation of exciting and challenging literature on the future. Much of it is serious, and not mere science fiction.[1] Moreover, both in the United States and, to a lesser degree, in Western Europe a number of systematic, scholarly efforts have been designed to project, predict, and possess what the future holds for us. Curiously, very little has been heard on this theme from the Communist World, even though Communist doctrinarians are the first to claim their nineteeth-century ideology holds a special passkey to the twenty-first century.

The work in progress indicates that men living in the developed world will undergo during the next several decades a mutation potentially as basic as that experienced through the slow process of evolution from animal to human experience. The difference, however, is that the process will be telescoped in time — and hence the shock effect of the change may be quite profound. Human conduct will become less spontaneous and less mysterious — more predetermined and subject to deliberate "programming." Man will increasingly possess the capacity to determine the sex of his children, to affect through drugs the extent of their intelligence and to modify and control their personalities. The human brain will acquire expanded powers, with computers becoming as routine an extension of man's reasoning as automobiles have been of man's mobility. The human body will be improved and its durability extended: some estimate that during the next century the average life-span could reach approximately 120 years.

These developments will have major social impact. The prolongation of life will alter our values, our career patterns, and our social relationships. New forms of social control may be needed to limit the indiscriminate exercise by individuals of their new powers. The possibility of extensive chemical mind-control, the danger of loss of individuality inherent in extensive transplantation, and the feasibility of manipulation of the genetic structure will call for a social definition of common criteria of restraint as well as of utilization. Scientists predict with some confidence that by the end of this century, computers will reason as well as man and will be able to engage in "creative" thought; wedded to robots or to "laboratory beings," they could act like humans. The makings of a most complex — and perhaps bitter — philosophical and political dialogue about the nature of man are self-evident in these developments.

Other discoveries and refinements will further alter society as we now know it. The information revolution, including extensive information storage, instant retrieval, and eventually push-button visual and sound availability of needed data in almost any private home, will transform the character of institutionalized collective education. The same techniques could serve to impose well-nigh total political surveillance on every citizen, putting into much sharper relief than is the case today the question of privacy. Cybernetics and automation will revolutionize working habits, with leisure becoming the practice and active work the exception — and a privilege reserved for the most talented. The achievement-oriented society might give way to the amusement-focused society, with essentially spectator spectacles (mass sports, TV) providing an opiate for increasingly purposeless masses.

But while for the masses life will grow longer and time will seem to expand, for the activist élite time will become a rare commodity. Indeed, even the élite's sense of time will alter. Already now speed dictates the pace of our lives — instead of the other way around. As the speed of transportation increases, largely by its own technological momentum, man discovers that he has no choice but to avail himself of that acceleration, either to keep up with others or because he thinks he can thus accomplish more. This will be especially true of the élite, for whom an expansion in leisure time does not seem to be in the cards. Thus as speed expands, time contracts — and the pressures on the élite increase.

By the end of this century the citizens of the more developed countries will live predominantly in cities — hence almost surrounded by man-made environment. Confronting nature could be to them what facing the elements was to our forefathers: meeting the unknown and not necessarily liking it. Enjoying a personal standard of living that (in some countries) may reach almost $10,000 per head, eating artificial food, speedily commuting from one corner of the country to work in another, in continual visual contact with their employer, government, or family, consulting their annual calendars to establish on which day it will rain or shine, our descendants will be shaped almost entirely by what they themselves create and control.

But even short of these far-reaching changes, the transformation that is now taking place is already creating a society increasingly unlike its industrial predecessor.[2] In the industrial society, technical knowledge was applied primarily to one specific end: the acceleration and improvement of production techniques. Social consequences were a later by-product of this paramount concern. In the technetronic society, scientific and technological knowledge, in addition to enhancing productive capabilities, quickly spills over to affect directly almost all aspects of life.

This is particularly evident in the case of the impact of communications and computers. Communications create an extraordinarily interwoven society, in continuous visual, audial, and increasingly close contact among almost all its members — electronically interacting, sharing instantly most intense social experiences, prompting far greater personal involvement, with their consciousnesses shaped in a sporadic manner fundamentally different (as McLuhan has noted) from the literate (or pamphleteering) mode of transmitting information, characteristic of the industrial age. The growing capacity for calculating instantly most complex interactions and the increasing availability of biochemical means of human control increase the potential scope of self-conscious direction, and thereby also the pressures to direct, to choose, and to change.

The consequence is a society that differs from the industrial one in a variety of economic, political, and social aspects. The following examples may be briefly cited to summarize some of the contrasts:

1. In an industrial society, the mode of production shifts from agriculture to industry, with the use of muscle and animals supplanted by machine operation. In the technetronic society, industrial employment yields to services, with automation and cybernetics replacing individual operation of machines.

2. Problems of employment and unemployment — not to speak of the earlier stage of the urban socialization of the postrural labor force — dominate the relationship between employers, labor, and the market in the industrial society; assuring minimum welfare to the new industrial masses is a source of major concern. In the emerging new society, questions relating to skill-obsolescence, security, vacations, leisure, and profit-sharing dominate the relationship; the matter of psychic well-being of millions of relatively secure but potentially aimless lower-middle class blue collar workers becomes a growing problem.

3. Breaking down traditional barriers to education, thus creating the basic point of departure for social advancement, is a major goal of social reformers in the industrial society. Education, available for limited and specific periods of time, is initially concerned with overcoming illiteracy, and subsequently with technical training, largely based on written, sequential reasoning. In the technetronic society, not only has education become universal but advanced training is available to almost all who have the basic talents. Quantity training is reinforced by far greater emphasis on quality selection. The basic problem is to discover the most effective techniques for the rational exploitation of social talent. Latest communication and calculating techniques are applied to that end. The educational process, relying much more on visual and audial devices, becomes extended in time, while the flow of new knowledge necessitates more and more frequent refresher studies.

4. In the industrial society social leadership shifts from the traditional rural-aristocratic to an urban "plutocratic" élite. Newly acquired wealth is its foundation, and intense competition the outlet — as well as the stimulus — for its energy. In the postindustrial technetronic society plutocratic pre-eminence comes under a sustained challenge from the political leadership which itself is increasingly permeated by individuals possessing special skills and intellectual talents. Knowledge becomes a tool of power, and the effective mobilization of talent an important way for acquiring power.

5. The university in an industrial society — rather in contrast to the medieval times — is an aloof ivory tower, the repository of irrelevant, even if respected wisdom, and, for only a brief time, the watering fountain for budding members of the established social élite. In the technetronic society, the university becomes an intensely involved *think-tank,* the source of much sustained political planning and social innovation.

6. The turmoil inherent in the shift from the rigidly traditional rural to urban existence engenders an inclination to seek total answers to social dilemmas, thus causing ideologies to thrive in the industrial society.[3] In the technetronic society, increasing ability to reduce social conflicts to quantifiable and measurable dimensions reinforces the trend toward a more pragmatic problem-solving approach to social issues.

7. The activization of hitherto passive masses makes for intense political conflicts in the industrial society over such matters as disenfranchisement and the right to vote. The issue of political participation is a crucial one. In the technetronic age, the question increasingly is one of ensuring real participation in decisions that seem too complex and too far-removed from the average citizen. Political alienation becomes a problem. Similarly, the issue of political equality of the sexes gives way to a struggle for the sexual equality of women. In the industrial society, woman — the operator of machines — ceases to be physically inferior to the male, a consideration of some importance in rural life, and she then begins to demand her political rights. In the emerging society, automation discriminates equally against males and females; intellectual talent is computable; the pill encourages sexual equality.

8 The newly enfranchised masses are coordinated in the industrial society through trade unions and political parties, and integrated by relatively simple and somewhat ideological programs. Moreover, political attitudes are influenced by appeals to nationalist sentiments, communicated through the massive growth of newspapers, relying, naturally, on native tongues. In the technetronic society, the trend would seem to be toward the aggregation of the individual support of millions of uncoordinated citizens, easily within the reach of magnetic and attractive personalities effectively exploiting the latest communication techniques to manipulate emotions and control reason. Reliance on TV — and hence the tendency to replace language with imagery, with the latter unlimited by national confines (and also including coverage for such matters as hunger in India or war scenes) — tends to create a somewhat more cosmopolitan, though highly impressionistic, involvement in global affairs.

9. Economic power in the industrial society tends to be personalized, either in the shape of great *entrepreneurs* like Henry Ford or bureaucratic industrializers like Kaganovich in Russia or Minc in Poland. The tendency toward depersonalization of economic power is stimulated in the next stage by the appearance of a highly complex interdependence between governmental institutions (including the military), scientific establishments, and industrial

organizations. As economic power becomes inseparably linked with political power, it becomes more invisible and the sense of individual futility increases.

10. Relaxation and escapism in the industrial society, in its more intense forms, is a carry-over from the rural drinking bout, in which intimate friends and family would join. Bars and saloons — or fraternities — strive to recreate the atmosphere of intimacy. In the technetronic society social life tends to be so atomized, even though communications (especially TV) make for unprecedented immediacy of social experience, that group intimacy cannot be re-created through the artificial stimulation of externally convivial group behavior. The new interest in drugs seeks to create intimacy through introspection, allegedly by expanding consciousness.

Eventually, these changes and many others, including the ones that affect much more directly the personality and quality of the human being itself, will make the technetronic society as different from the industrial as the industrial became from the agrarian.

THE AMERICAN TRANSITION

America is today in the midst of a transition. U.S. society is leaving the phase of spontaneity and is entering a more self-conscious stage; ceasing to be an industrial society, it is becoming the first technetronic one. This is at least in part the cause for much of the current tensions and violence.

Spontaneity made for an almost automatic optimism about the future, about the "American miracle," about justice and happiness for all. This myth prompted social blinders to the various aspects of American life that did not fit the optimistic mold, particularly the treatment of the Negro and the persistence of pockets of deprivation. Spontaneity involved a faith in the inherent goodness of the American socioeconomic dynamic: as America developed, grew, became richer, problems that persisted or appeared would be solved.

This phase is ending. Today, American society is troubled and some parts of it are even tormented. The social blinders are being ripped off — and a sense of inadequacy is becoming more wide-spread. The spread of literacy, and particularly the access to college and universities of about 40 per cent of the youth, has created a new stratum — one which reinforces the formerly isolated urban intellectuals — a stratum not willing to tolerate either social blinders or sharing the complacent belief in the spontaneous goodness of American social change.

Yet it is easier to know what is wrong than to indicate what ought to be done. The difficulty is not only revealed by the inability of the new social rebels to develop a concrete and meaningful program. It is magnified by the novelty of America's problem. Turning to nineteenth-century ideologies is not the answer — and it is symptomatic that the "New Left" has found it most difficult to apply the available, particularly Marxist, doctrines to the new reality. Indeed, its emphasis on human rights, the evils of deperson-alization, the dangers inherent in big government — so responsive to the felt psychological needs — contain strong parallels to more conservative notions about the place and sanctity of the individual in society.

In some ways, there is an analogy here between the "New Left" and the searching attitude of various disaffected groups in early nineteenth-century Europe, reacting to the first strains of the in-dustrial age. Not fully comprehending its meaning, not quite certain where it was heading — yet sensitive to the miseries and oppor-tunities it was bringing — many Europeans strove desperately to adapt earlier, eighteenth-century doctrines to the new reality. It was finally Marx who achieved what appeared to many millions a mean-ingful synthesis, combining utopian idealism about the future of the industrial age with a scorching critique of its present.

The search for meaning is characteristic of the present American scene. It could portend most divisive and bitter ideological conflicts — especially as intellectual disaffection becomes linked with the increasing bitterness of the deprived Negro masses. If carried to its extreme, this could bring to America a phase of violent, intolerant, and destructive civil strife, combining ideological and racial in-tolerance.

However, it seems unlikely that a unifying ideology of political action, capable of mobilizing large-scale loyalty, can emerge in the manner that Marxism arose in response to the industrial era. Unlike even Western Europe or Japan — not to speak of Soviet Russia — where the consequences and the impact of the industrial process are still reshaping political, social, and economic life, in America science and technology (particularly as socially applied through communications and increasing computarization, both off-springs of the industrial age) are already more important in influencing the social behavior of a society that has moved past its industrial phase. Science and technology are notoriously unsympathetic to simple, absolute formulas. In the technetronic society there may be room for pragmatic, even impatient, idealism, but hardly for doctrinal utopianism.

At the same time, it is already evident that a resolution of some of the unfinished business of the industrial era will be rendered more acute. For example, the Negro should have been integrated into U.S. society *during* the American industrial revolution. Yet that revolution came before America, even if not the Negro, was ready for full integration. If the Negro had been only an economic legacy of the preindustrial age, perhaps he could have integrated more effectively. Today, the more advanced urban-industrial regions of America, precisely because they are moving into a new and more complex phase, requiring even more developed social skills, are finding it very difficult to integrate the Negro, both a racial minority and America's only "feudal legacy." Paradoxically, it can be argued that the American South today stands a better long-range chance of fully integrating the Negro: American consciousness is changing, the Negro has stirred, and the South is beginning to move into the industrial age. The odds are that it may take the Negro along with it.

Whatever the outcome, American society is the one in which the great questions of our time will be first tested through practice. Can the individual and science coexist, or will the dynamic momentum of the latter fundamentally alter the former? Can man, living in the scientific age, grow in intellectual depth and philosophical meaning, and thus in his personal liberty too? Can the institutions of political democracy be adapted to the new conditions sufficiently quickly to meet the crises, yet without debasing their democratic character?

The challenge in its essence involves the twin dangers of fragmentation and excessive control. A few examples. Symptoms of alienation and depersonalization are already easy to find in American society. Many Americans feel "less free"; this feeling seems to be connected with their loss of "purpose"; freedom implies choice of action, and action requires an awareness of goals. If the present transition of America to the technetronic age achieves no personally satisfying fruits, the next phase may be one of sullen withdrawal from social and political involvement, a flight from social and political responsibility through "inner-emigration." Political frustration could increase the difficulty of absorbing and internalizing rapid environmental changes, thereby prompting increasing psychic instability.

At the same time, the capacity to assert social and political control over the individual will vastly increase. As I have already noted, it will soon be possible to assert almost continuous surveillance over every citizen and to maintain up-to-date, complete files, containing even most personal information about the health or personal behavior of the citizen, in addition to more customary data. These files will be subject to instantaneous retrieval by the authorities.

Moreover, the rapid pace of change will put a premium on anticipating events and planning for them. Power will gravitate into the hands of those who control the information and can correlate it most rapidly. Our existing *post*crisis management institutions will probably be increasingly supplanted by *pre*crisis management institutions, the task of which will be to identify in advance likely social crises and to develop programs to cope with them. This could encourage tendencies during the next several decades toward a technocratic dictatorship, leaving less and less room for political procedures as we now know them.

Finally, looking ahead to the end of this century, the possibility of biochemical mind-control and genetic tinkering with man, including eventually the creation of beings that will function like men — and reason like them as well — could give rise to the most difficult questions. According to what criteria can such controls be applied? What is the distribution of power between the individual and society with regard to means that can altogether alter man? What is the social and political status of artificial beings, if they begin to approach man in their performance and creative capacities? (One dares not ask, what if they begin to "outstrip man" -— something not beyond the pale of possibility during the next century?)

Yet it would be highly misleading to construct a one-sided picture, a new Orwellian piece of science fiction. Many of the changes transforming American society augur well for the future and allow at least some optimism about this society's capacity to adapt to the requirements of the metamorphic age.

Thus, in the political sphere, the increased flow of information and more efficient techniques of coordination need not necessarily prompt greater concentration of power within some ominous control agency located at the governmental apex. Paradoxically, these developments also make possible greater devolution of authority and responsibility to the lower levels of government and society. The division of power has traditionally posed the problems of inefficiency, coordination, and dispersal of authority; but today the new communications and computer techniques make possible both increased authority at the lower levels and almost instant national coordination. It is very likely that state and local government will be strengthened in the next ten years, and many functions now the responsibility of the federal government will be assumed by them.[4]

The devolution of financial responsibility to lower echelons may encourage both the flow of better talent and greater local participation in more important local decision-making. National coordination and local participation could thus be wedded by the new systems of coordination. This has already been tried successfully by some large businesses. This development would also have the desirable effect of undermining the appeal of any new integrating ideologies that may arise; for ideologies thrive only as long as there is an acute need for abstract responses to large and remote problems.

It is also a hopeful sign that improved governmental performance, and its increased sensitivity to social needs is being stimulated by the growing involvement in national affairs of what Kenneth Boulding has called the Educational and Scientific Establishment (EASE). The university at one time, during the Middle Ages, was a key social institution. Political leaders leaned heavily on it for literate confidants and privy councillors; a rare commodity in those days. Later divorced from reality, academia in recent years has made a grand re-entry into the world of action.

Today, the university is the creative eye of the massive communications complex, the source of much strategic planning, domestic and international. Its engagement in the world is encouraging the appearance of a new breed of politicians-intellectuals, men who make it a point to mobilize and draw on the most expert, scientific, and academic advice in the development of their political programs. This, in turn, stimulates public awareness of the value of expertise — and, again in turn, greater political competition in exploiting it.

A profound change in the intellectual community itself is inherent in this development. The largely humanist-oriented, occasionally ideologically-minded intellectual-dissenter, who saw his role largely in terms of proffering social critiques, is rapidy being displaced either by experts and specialists, who become involved in special governmental undertakings, or by the generalists-integrators, who become in effect house-ideologues for those in power, providing over-all intellectual integration for disparate actions. A community of organization-oriented, application-minded intellectuals, relating itself more effectively to the political system than their predecessors, serves to introduce into the political system concerns broader than those likely to be generated by that system itself and perhaps more relevant than those articulated by outside critics.[5]

The expansion of knowledge, and the entry into sociopolitical life of the intellectual community, has the further effect of making education an almost continuous process. By 1980, not only will approximately two-thirds of U.S. urban dwellers be college trained, but it is almost certain that systematic "élite-retraining" will be standard in the political system. It will be normal for every high official both to be engaged in almost continuous absorption of new techniques and knowledge and to take periodic retraining. The adoption of compulsory elementary education was a revolution brought on by the industrial age. In the new technetronic society, it will be equally necessary to require everyone at a sufficiently responsible post to take, say, two years of retraining every ten years. (Perhaps there will even be a constitutional amendment, requiring a President-elect to spend at least a year getting himself educationally up-to-date.) Otherwise, it will not be possible either to keep up with, or absorb, the new knowledge.

Given diverse needs, it is likely that the educational system will undergo a fundamental change in structure. Television-computer consoles, capable of bringing most advanced education to the home, will permit extensive and continuous adult re-education. On the more advanced levels, it is likely that government agencies and corporations will develop — and some have already begun to do so — their own advanced educational systems, shaped to their special needs. As education becomes both a continuum, and even more application-oriented, its organizational framework will be redesigned to tie it directly to social and political action.

It is quite possible that a society increasingly geared to learning will be able to absorb more resiliently the expected changes in social and individual life. Mechanization of labor and the introduction of robots will reduce the chores that keep millions busy doing things that they dislike doing. The increasing GNP (which could reach approximately $10,000 per capita per year), linked with educational advance, could prompt among those less involved in social management and less interested in scientific development a wave of interest in the cultural and humanistic aspects of life, in addition to purely hedonistic preoccupations. But even the latter would serve as a social valve, reducing tensions and political frustration. Greater control over external environment could make for easier, less uncertain existence.

But the key to successful adaptation to the new conditions is in the effective selection, distribution, and utilization of social talent. If the industrial society can be said to have developed through a struggle for survival of the fittest, the technetronic society — in order to prosper — requires the effective mobilization of the ablest. Objective and systematic criteria for the selection of those with the greatest gifts will have to be developed, and the maximum opportunity for their training and advancement provided. The new society will require enormous talents — as well as a measure of philosophical wisdom — to manage and integrate effectively the expected changes. Otherwise, the dynamic of change could chaotically dictate the patterns of social change.

Fortunately, American society is becoming more conscious not only of the principle of equal opportunity for all but of special opportunity for the singularly talented few. Never truly an aristocratic state (except for some pockets such as the South and New England), never really subject to ideological or charismatic leadership, gradually ceasing to be a plutocratic-oligarchic society, the U.S.A. is becoming something which may be labeled the "meritocratic democracy." It combines continued respect for the popular will with an increasing role in the key decision-making institutions of individuals with special intellectual and scientific attainments. The educational and social systems are making it increasingly attractive and easy for those meritocratic few to develop to the fullest their special potential. The recruitment and advancement of social talent is yet to extend to the poorest and the most underprivileged, but that too is coming. No one can tell whether this will suffice to meet the unfolding challenge, but the increasingly cultivated and programmed American society, led by a meritocratic democracy, may stand a better chance.

THE TRAUMA OF CONFRONTATION

For the world at large, the appearance of the new technetronic society could have the paradoxical effect of creating more distinct worlds on a planet that is continuously shrinking because of the communications revolution. While the scientific-technological change will inevitably have some spill-over, not only will the gap between the developed and the underdeveloped worlds probably become wider — especially in the more measurable terms of economic indices — but a *new one* may be developing *within* the industrialized and urban world.

The fact is that America, having left the industrial phase, is today entering a distinct historical era: and one different from that of Western Europe and Japan. This is prompting subtle and still indefinable changes in the American psyche, providing the psychocultural bases for the more evident political disagreements between the two sides of the Atlantic. To be sure, there are pockets of innovation or retardation on both sides. Sweden shares with America the problems of leisure, psychic well-being, purposelessness; while Mississippi is experiencing the confrontation with the industrial age in a way not unlike some parts of South-Western Europe. But I believe the broad generalization still holds true: Europe and America are no longer in the same historical era.

What makes America unique in our time is that it is the first society to experience the future. The confrontation with the new — which will soon include much of what I have outlined — is part of the daily American experience. For better or for worse, the rest of the world learns what is in store for it by observing what happens in the U.S.A.: in the latest scientific discoveries in space, in medicine, or the electric toothbrush in the bathroom; in pop art or LSD, air conditioning or air pollution, old-age problems or juvenile delinquency. The evidence is more elusive in such matters as music, style, values, social mores; but there, too, the term "Americanization" obviously defines the source. Today, America is *the* creative society; the others, consciously and unconsciously, are emulative.

American scientific leadership is particularly strong in the so-called "frontier" industries, involving the most advanced fields of science. It has been estimated that approximately 80 per cent of all scientific and technical discoveries made during the last few decades originated in the United States. About 75 per cent of the world's computers operate in United States; the American lead in lasers is even more marked; examples of American scientific lead are abundant.

There is reason to assume that this leadership will continue. America has four times as many scientists and research workers as the countries of the European Economic Community combined; three-and-a-half times as many as the Soviet Union. The brain-drain is almost entirely one-way. The United States is also spending more on research: seven times as much as the E.E.C. countries, three-and-a-half times as much as the Soviet Union. Given the fact that scientific development is a dynamic process, it is likely that the gap will widen.[6]

On the social level, American innovation is most strikingly seen in the manner in which the new meritocratic élite is taking over American life, utilizing the universities, exploiting the latest techniques of communications, harnessing as rapidly as possible the most recent technological devices. Technetronics dominate American life, but so far nobody else's. This is bound to have social and political — and therefore also psychological — consequences, stimulating a psychocultural gap in the developed world.

At the same time, the backward regions of the world are becoming more, rather than less, poor in relation to the developed world. It can be roughly estimated that the per capita income of the underdeveloped world is approximately ten times lower than of America and Europe (and twenty-five times of America itself). By the end of the century, the ratio may be about fifteen-to-one (or possibly thirty-to-one in the case of the U.S.), with the backward nations *at best* approaching the present standard of the very poor European nations but in many cases (e.g., India) probably not even attaining that modest level.

The social élites of these regions, however, will quite naturally tend to assimilate and emulate, as much as their means and power permit, the life-styles of the most advanced world, with which they are, and increasingly will be, in close vicarious contact through global television, movies, travel, education, and international magazines. The international gap will thus have a domestic reflection, with the masses, given the availability even in most backward regions of transistorized radios (and soon television), becoming more and more intensely aware of their deprivation.

It is difficult to conceive how in that context democratic institutions (derived largely from Western experience — but typical only of the more stable and wealthy Western nations) will endure in a country like India, or develop elsewhere. The foreseeable future is more likely to see a turn toward personal dictatorships and some unifying doctrines, in the hope that the combination of the two may preserve the minimum stability necessary for social-economic development. The problem, however, is that whereas in the past ideologies of change gravitated from the developed world to the less, in a way stimulating imitation of the developed world (as was the case with Communism), today the differences between the two worlds are so pronounced that it is difficult to conceive a new ideological wave originating from the developed world, where the tradition of utopian thinking is generally declining.

With the widening gap dooming any hope of imitation, the more likely development is an ideology of rejection of the developed world. Racial hatred could provide the necessary emotional force, exploited by xenophobic and romantic leaders. The writings of Frantz Fanon — violent and racist — are a good example. Such ideologies of rejection, combining racialism with nationalism, would further reduce the chances of meaningful regional cooperation, so essential if technology and science are to be effectively applied. They would certainly widen the existing psychological and emotional gaps. Indeed, one might ask at that point: who is the truer repository of that indefinable quality we call human? The technologically dominant and conditioned technetron, increasingly trained to adjust to leisure, or the more "natural" and backward agrarian, more and more dominated by racial passions and continuously exhorted to work harder, even as his goal of the good life becomes more elusive?

The result could be a modern version on a global scale of the old rural-urban dichotomy. In the past, the strains produced by the shift from an essentially agricultural economy to a more urban one contributed much of the impetus for revolutionary violence.[7] Applied on a global scale, this division could give substance to Lin Piao's bold thesis that:

Taking the entire globe, if North America and Western Europe can be called "the cities of the world," then Asia, Africa and Latin America constitute "the rural areas of the world."... In a sense, the contemporary world revolution also presents a picture of the encirclement of cities by the rural areas.

In any case, even without envisaging such a dichotomic confrontation, it is fair to say that the underdeveloped regions will be facing increasingly grave problems of political stability and social survival. Indeed (to use a capsule formula), in the developed world, the nature of man as man is threatened; in the underdeveloped, society is. The interaction of the two could produce chaos.

To be sure, the most advanced states will possess ever more deadly means of destruction, possibly even capable of nullifying the consequences of the nuclear proliferation that appears increasingly inevitable. Chemical and biological weapons, death rays, neutron bombs, nerve gases, and a host of other devices, possessed in all their sophisticated variety (as seems likely) only by the two super-states, may impose on the world a measure of stability. Nonetheless, it seems unlikely, given the rivalry between the two principal powers, that a full-proof system against international violence can be established. Some local wars between the weaker, nationalistically more aroused, poorer nations may occasionally erupt — resulting perhaps even in the total nuclear extinction of one or several smaller nations? — before greater international control is imposed in the wake of the universal moral shock thereby generated.

The underlying problem, however, will be to find a way of avoiding somehow the widening of the cultural and psychosocial gap inherent in the growing differentiation of the world. Even with gradual differentiation throughout human history, it was not until the industrial revolution that sharp differences between societies began to appear. Today, some nations still live in conditions not unlike pre-Christian times; many no different than in the medieval age. Yet soon a few will live in ways so new that it is now difficult to imagine their social and individual ramifications. If the developed world takes a leap — as seems inescapably the case — into a reality that is even more different from ours today than ours is from an Indian village, the gap and its accompanying strains will not narrow.

On the contrary, the instantaneous electronic intermeshing of mankind will make for an intense confrontation, straining social and international peace. In the past, differences were "livable" because of time and distance that separated them. Today, these differences are actually widening while technetronics are eliminating the two insulants of time and distance. The resulting trauma could create almost entirely different perspectives on life, with insecurity, envy, and hostility becoming the dominant emotions for increasingly large numbers of people. A three-way split into rural-backward, urban-industrial, and technetronic ways of life can only further divide man, intensify the existing difficulties to global understanding, and give added vitality to latent or existing conflicts.

The pace of American development both widens the split within mankind and contains the seeds for a constructive response. However, neither military power nor material wealth, both of which America possesses in abundance, can be used directly in responding to the onrushing division in man's thinking, norms, and character. Power, at best, can assure only a relatively stable external environment: the tempering or containing of the potential global civil war; wealth can grease points of socioeconomic friction, thereby facilitating development. But as man — especially in the most advanced societies — moves increasingly into the phase of controlling and even creating his environment, increasing attention will have to be given to giving man meaningful content — to improving the quality of life for man *as man*.

Man has never really tried to use science in the realm of his value systems. Ethical thinking is hard to change, but history demonstrates that it does change.... Man does, in limited ways, direct his very important and much more rapid psychosocial education. The evolution of such things as automobiles, airplanes, weapons, legal institutions, corporations, universities, and democratic governments are examples of progressive evolution in the course of time. We have, however, never really tried deliberately to create a better society for man *qua* man....[8]

The urgent need to do just that may compel America to redefine its global posture. During the remainder of this century, given the perspective on the future I have outlined here, America is likely to become less concerned with "fighting communism" or creating "a world safe for diversity" than with helping to develop a common response with the rest of mankind to the implications of a truly new era. This will mean making the massive diffusion of scientific-technological knowledge a principal focus of American involvement in world affairs.

To some extent, the U.S. performs that role already — simply by being what it is. The impact of its reality and its global involvement prompts emulation. The emergence of vast international corporations, mostly originating in the United States, makes for easier transfer of skills, management techniques, marketing procedures, and scientific-technological innovations. The appearance of these corporations in the Europe market has done much to stimulate Europeans to consider urgently the need to integrate their resources and to accelerate the pace of their research and development.

Similarly, returning graduates from American universities have prompted an organizational and intellectual revolution in the academic life of their countries. Changes in the academic life of Britain, Germany, Japan, more recently France, and (to even a greater extent) in the less developed countries, can be traced to the influence of U.S. educational institutions. Indeed, the leading technological institute in Turkey conducts its lectures in "American" and is deliberately imitating, not only in approach but in student-professor relationships, U.S. patterns. Given developments in modern communications, is it not only a matter of time before students at Columbia University and, say, the University of Teheran will be watching, *simultaneously,* the same lecturer?

The appearance of a universal intellectual élite, one that shares certain common values and aspirations, will somewhat compensate for the widening differentiation among men and societies. But it will not resolve the problem posed by that differentiation. In many backward nations tension between what is and what can be will be intensified. Moreover, as Kenneth Boulding observed:

The network of electronic communication is inevitably producing a world super-culture, and the relations between this super-culture and the more traditional national and regional cultures of the past remains the great question mark of the next fifty years.[9]

That "super-culture," strongly influenced by American life, with its own universal electronic-computer language, will find it difficult to relate itself to "the more traditional and regional cultures," especially if the basic gap continues to widen.

To cope with that gap, a gradual change in diplomatic style and emphasis may have to follow the redefined emphasis of America's involvement in world affairs. Professional diplomacy will have to yield to intellectual leadership. With government negotiating directly — or quickly dispatching the negotiators — there will be less need for ambassadors who are resident diplomats and more for ambassadors who are capable of serving as creative interpreters of the new age, willing to engage in a meaningful dialogue with the host intellectual community and concerned with promoting the widest possible dissemination of available knowledge. Theirs will be the task to stimulate and to develop scientific-technological programs of cooperation.

International cooperation will be necessary in almost every facet of life: to reform and to develop more modern educational systems, to promote new sources of food supply, to accelerate economic development, to stimulate technological growth, to control climate, to disseminate new medical knowledge. However, because the new élites have a vested interest in their new nation-states and because of the growing xenophobia among the masses in the third world, the nation-state will remain for a long time the primary focus of loyalty, especially for newly liberated and economically backward peoples. To predict loudly its death, and to act often as if it were dead, could prompt — as it did partially in Europe — an adverse reaction from those whom one would wish to influence. Hence, regionalism will have to be promoted with due deference to the symbolic meaning of national sovereignty — and preferably by encouraging those concerned themselves to advocate regional approaches.

Even more important will be the stimulation, for the first time in history on a global scale, of the much needed dialogue on what it is about man's life that we wish to safeguard or to promote, and on the relevance of existing moral systems to an age that cannot be fitted into the narrow confines of fading doctrines. The search for new directions — going beyond the tangibles of economic development — could be an appropriate subject for a special world congress, devoted to the technetronic and philosophical problems of the coming age. To these issues no one society, however advanced, is in a position to provide an answer.

NOTES

1. Perhaps the most useful single source is to be found in the Summer 1967 issue of *Daedalus,* devoted entirely to *"Toward the Year 2000: Work in Progress."* The introduction by Professor Daniel Bell, chairman of the American Academy's Commission on the Year 2000 (of which the present writer is also a member) summarizes some of the principal literature on the subject.
2. See Daniel Bell's pioneering "Notes on the Post-Industrial Society," *The Public Interest,* Nos. 6 and 7, 1967.
3. The American exception to this rule was due to the absence of the feudal tradition, a point well developed by Louis Hartz in his work, *The Liberal Tradition in America* (1955).
4. It is noteworthy that the U.S. Army has so developed its control systems that it is not uncommon for sergeants to call in and coordinate massive air strikes and artillery fire — a responsibility of colonels during World War II.
5. However, there is a danger in all this that ought not to be neglected. Intense involvement in applied knowledge could gradually prompt a waning of the tradition of learning for the sake of learning. The intellectual community, including the university, could become another, "industry," meeting social needs as the market dictates, with the intellectuals reaching for the highest material and political rewards. Concern with power, prestige, and the good life could mean an end to the aristocratic ideal of intellectual detachment and the disinterested search for truth.
6. In the Soviet case, rigid compartmentalization between secret military research and industrial research has had a particularly

sterile effect of inhibiting spill-over from weapons research into industrial application.

7. See Barrington Moore's documentation of this in his pioneering study *Social Origins of Dictatorship and Democracy* (1967).

8. Hudson Hoagland, "Biology, Brains, and Insight," *Columbia University Forum,* Summer 1967.

9. Kenneth Boulding, "Expecting the Unexpected," *Prospective Changes in Society by 1980* (1960).

9: Robots and Rebels

Arthur P. Mendel

... The essential accusation of the Great Refusal is
directed against the subordination of human experience to the economic processes of the consumer society and its increasingly more
absurd products, to the aggressive militarism that at least in our
case has become so tightly interwoven with this society, and to the
gigantic, impersonal organizations through which it all functions.

The Great Refusal may be either active or passive. It is active
when the rebels insist on action that has clearly human, moral, or
creative value: they may be activists in the more publicized civil
rights movement, Peace Corps, community action committees, or
antiwar demonstrations, or in the more private ways in which they
choose careers of social service or aesthetic creativity rather than
those associated with traditional success and the pursuit of power.
There is a drop in engineering school enrollment. Law firms raise
beginning salaries sharply to counter the decline in applicants.
Scientists forgo the lush military and commercial contracts. And

From *The New Republic,* January 11, 1969, pp. 18-19. Copyright 1969, Harrison-Blaine
of New Jersey, Inc.

should they willy-nilly find themselves caught in the commercial-industrial world, the rebels undermine its essential ethos, make it more mellow and humane. The Great Refusal is passive when the rebels just let go, step down from the treadmill of time and achievement into a timeless present, the residence of sensual and contemplative delight. Here, too, there are the dramatic and the more covert expressions, both the spectacular hippies and the more reticent but more important millions who are finding the time that was supposedly never there to enjoy the books, music, sports, arts and crafts, travel, open companionships, and all the other joys that economic man could only skimpily, grudgingly, and guiltily allow himself. For technetronic man much of this may be intolerable hedonism; but for "man *as man*" it is the leap to freedom that utopians envisioned and that centuries of technological achievement and human self-sacrifice have at last prepared.

As long as deprivation and scarcity characterized social existence, as long as economic progress continued to mean a struggle for securing the material basis for social existence, these opponents, as Brzezinski correctly says, were powerless and easily overcome. What Brzezinski fails to see is that the achievement of the affluent society, the victory of science and technology, the assurance of the material conditions of life comprise a qualitative change that radically alters all this. From being innocuous irritants, the opposing forces are in fact acquiring, through the very processes of the system they oppose, the power to dethrone economic man, to soften then dissolve the taut constraints, the repressions and obligations that have welded generations of mankind with other "factors of production" into our dismal social factory....

The Great Refusal is exactly the kind of revolutionary movement one would expect to emerge from the affluent society. It is precisely the Great Refusal that focuses on the "psychic" problems, the problems of leisure, of "giving man meaningful content" and "improving the quality of life for man *as man*," on the concerns that Brzezinski himself realizes are among the most compelling that men and women in the advanced societies face. And it is a revolution that draws together the generations, belieing too hasty assertions about the generation gap. The young have learned many of their lessons, and have found much of their voice, from a long list of adult social critics, past and present; names like Marcuse, Goodman, De Grazia, and Galbraith are only the most recent of a long heritage. But more important still, the rebellious youth have found varying degrees of support from their own parents, who, while too rigidly formed, too "up-tight," too well "programmed" to abandon the compulsive style themselves, nevertheless sense that their children are right in trying to do so, that the affluent society has removed the risks such autonomy used to entail, that their children need not run as scared as they did.

It is absurd for politicians, judges, scholars, and elder statesmen to scold the parents for "permissiveness": this misses the whole point of what is going on. Moreover, the weakness of the parental position in this confrontation with their children is all the greater because of the essential ambivalence that has always existed in our economized life, our deep belief that it is somehow sinful to strive obsessively for material accumulation, to compete aggressively against our fellow men, to ignore the poor and to condone mendacity and hypocrisy as socially, politically, or economically necessary. What can the parents say to the children who come urging love instead of hate, service instead of self-aggrandizement, beauty instead of fashion, communion instead of competition? How can they denounce those who have initiated and carried through the civil-rights movement and the antiwar demonstrations, those who have made such noble enterprises as the Peace Corps a reality, and who today strive through their free universities and in other ways to preserve liberal education, education that concerns human, existential questions rather than the further refinement of already supersophisticated computers, the better marketing of lipstick, or the concoction of more deadly nerve gases?

Still, if the youth have found guidance and support among the adult world, it is nonetheless true that they are the effective vanguard of the "new class" and its Great Refusal. It is in these years of late adolescence, the years between the dependency of childhood and the dependency of adult, family responsibilities, that one is psychologically ready and socially able to stand outside of one's society and the image of it in oneself and judge them both. And to this extent the rebellion is part of the familiar and repeated assault of each generation of youth against the older authorities, both a necessary step toward adult autonomy and a last defense of youthful spontaneity and diversity. However, and this, I think, is the crux of it all, the meaning of the Great Refusal and of the leading role of youth in it, this customary adolescent reluctance to give up freedom for constrained roles or critical honesty for socially required hypocrisy, now coincides with the possibilities that affluence is beginning to allow society as a whole — for the first time in human history — to preserve or regain such freedom and honesty. . Youth no longer speaks only for itself: it defines an era. And, understandably, it is at the universities of the country where this definition takes form. Not only because it is here that so many of the sensitive, thoughtful, and articulate youth find themselves, but also because it is here that they learn to look critically at different societies and values, including their own, to see truth rather than social conventions, and is here they acquire an arsenal of perennial human values with which to sustain their struggle for the good society. . . .

As I have argued, there is good reason to think that it is the rebels of the Great Refusal and not the technetronic servitors who speak for the future. I have in mind the increasing number of youth in universities and their growing role throughout the society; the spread among them of all sorts of cults for letting go and their leading involvement in all the movements opposed to Brzezinski's utopia; the revival among the social sciences of personalist, subjectivist approaches in opposition to the heretofore dominant behaviorists; the spread of the humanistic psychology movement; the not-so-coincidental upsurge of anthropological studies of primitive societies, religious studies in mythology, and historians' interest in aristocracies; the richly emotional qualities of contemporary art; the leisure and sexual-sensual liberation; the growing influence of the underground church; the ubiquitous sprouting of small groups of all sorts where personal communion is rediscovered. It is mainly a quiet revolution, one without the programs and leadership that Brzezinski's twentieth-century mind considers prerequisite for an historically relevant revolution. It is not waiting for the cataclysmic confrontation that Marcuse, repeating Marx's error, seems to think necessary for this coming social transformation. It is taking place now, gradually changing the face of our society, the quality of our thought and experience, and the character of our behavior.

The Library

COLLEGE of MARIN

Kentfield, California

 PRINTED IN U.S.A.

COM

Index

Acheson, Dean, 73, 74
Age of Longing (Koestler), 82
87
Anabaptists, 84
Animal Farm (Orwell), 87
Anti-utopianism, twentieth century, 81-89
Ape and Essence (Huxley), 82, 87
Asimov, Isaac, 86, 89
Auden, W. H., 23
Automation, 129

"Bald Soprano, The" (Ionesco), 3
Barbary Shore (Mailer), 6, 24
Bell, Daniel, 22, 26, 149
Bellamy, Edward, 33
Bendix, Reinhard, 125
Berdyaev, Nikolai, 81
Boguslaw, Robert, 26
Boulding, Kenneth E., 27, 139, 147, 150
Bradbury, Ray, 9, 86, 88

Brave New World (Huxley), 9, 16-17, 25, 72, 77, 81, 82, 85, 87, 104
Brown, Norman O., 15, 27
Brzezinski, Zbigniew, 20-22, 26, 127-150, 152, 154-155
Buber, Martin, 27, 124
Burkhardt, Jacob, 96, 97
Burke, Edmund, 98
Butler, Samuel, 33

Capek, Karel, 83, 84, 87
Carstairs, M., 56
Catholic Church, 45, 89
Change, 8-11, 16, 59, 103-104, 107, 120-121, 127-149
Character, formation of, 16
Chesterton, G. K., 82
Christianity, 47, 61
Clecak, Peter, 25
Cobb, Edith, 52, 56
Cohn, Norman, 27
Communism, 19, 47, 61, 100, 128
Conservatism, 117-118

157

Coser, Lewis, 126
Courage, 17-19
Crucible Island (Pallen), 84
Cybernetics, 129

Daedalus, 23, 26, 149
Dahrendorf, Ralf, 7, 8, 24, 103-126
Darwin, Charles, 9
Death, 5-6
Democracy, 13, 57, 58, 61, 63-64, 74, 75
Deviance, 111-112
Dostoyevsky, Fyodor, 27, 60
Doxiades, Constantinos A., 27
Duhamel, Georges, 101

Education, 12, 14, 15, 86
   Technetronic Age and, 131-132, 140
Efficiency, 77-80
Eliot, T. S., 71
End of Eternity (Asimov), 89
Engels, Frederick, 19, 24, 25
Erikson, E. H., 42, 56
Eros and Civilization (Marcuse), 5, 24

Family, 16, 112
Fanon, Frantz, 144
Ferenczi, S., 33
Ferkiss, Victor C., 27
Forster, E. M., 27
Fourier, Charles, 16, 17
Frank, L. K., 56
Freedom, 12, 57-75, 86, 137
"Freedom and the Control of Men" (Skinner), 12
Freud, Sigmund, 16
Friedman, Milton, 110, 124
Frost, Robert, 36

Galbraith, John Kenneth, 153
Gerber, R., 124

Gesell, A., 42, 56
Gheorghiu, Virgil, 82, 83
Godwin, William, 35
Goethe, J. W. von, 87
Golden Age, 43
Golffing, Barbara, 24, 29-39
Golffing, Francis, 24, 27, 29-39
Goodman, P., 153
Great Ball of Wax (Mead), 86
Great Refusal, 151-155
Greener than Grass (Moore), 86
Gregory, Owen, 84, 86
Grey-Walter, W., 56
Gulliver's Travels, 84

Hacker, Andrew, 25
Haldane, J. B. S., 33
Halévy, Daniel, 86
Harrison, G. R., 56
Hartz, Louis, 149
Hegel, G. W. F., 120
Hendrix, G., 56
Heraclitus, 112
Heroism, 16-18
Hillegas, Mark R., 27
Historicism, 20, 21
Hitler, Adolf, 74
Hoagland, Hudson, 150
Holmes, Oliver Wendell, 73
Horsburgh, H. J. N., 27
Humanism, 22, 58
Huxley, Aldous, 9, 16-17, 25, 33, 72, 77, 78, 81, 82, 83, 87, 104, 105
Huxley, T. H. 71

Ilg, F., 42, 56
Industrial Revolution, 95, 136
Inhelder, Barbel, 42, 52, 56
Ionesco, Eugene, 3-4, 6, 24
Iron Heel (London), 84, 86

James, William, 27
Jehovah's Witnesses, 49

Jencks, Christopher, 17, 77-80
Jerusalem, 43-44
Jews, 49

Kahn, Herman, 26
Kateb, George, 1-24
Keats, John, 22
Keller, D. N., 86
Khrushchev, Nikita, 99
Koestler, Arthur, 82
Krutch, Joseph Wood, 25, 68, 70, 71

Lange, 110, 125
Leibniz, 31
Lenin, V. I., 27, 104, 108, 127
Lincoln, Abraham, 68
Lippmann, Walter, 27
Lipset, S. M., 125
London, Jack, 84
"Looking Back on the Spanish War" (Orwell), 4, 24
Lowenfeld, Margaret, 42, 56

Mailer, Norman, 4, 6, 24, 26
Mannheim, Karl, 27, 124
Manuel, Frank E., 27
Mao Tse-tung, 13
Marcel, Gabriel, 83
Marcus Aurelius, 59
Marcuse, Herbert, 5, 6, 15, 24, 27, 153, 155
Marshall, T. H., 115, 125
Marshall Plan, 62
Marx, Karl, 6, 19-21, 24, 25, 104, 111, 125, 155
Marxism, 100
McDermott, John, 26
McLuhan, Marshall, 131
Mead, Margaret, 24, 27, 41-56
Mead, S., 86
Measure of Man, The (Krutch), 68

Meccania—The Super-State (Gregory), 84
Mendel, Arthur P., 22, 151-155
Merton, Robert K., 115, 125
Michael, Donald N., 26
Mill, John Stuart, 4
Modern Utopia, A (Wells), 7, 9, 17, 24, 123
Monadology, 31
Moore, Barrington, Jr., 28, 150
Moore, Ward, 86
More, Sir Thomas, 31, 36
Morris, C., 56
Morris, William, 8, 30-31, 34
Mumford, Lewis, 28, 82, 124

Nadeau, Maurice, 88
Napoleon of Notting Hill, The (Chesterton), 82
Nazis, 87
Negley, Glenn, 28
New City, The (Fialko), 86
"New Left," 135
"News from Nowhere" (Morris), 8
1984 (Orwell), 72, 82, 87, 103
Nirvana, 44

Oneida community, 16
Open Society and Its Enemies (Popper), 107
Original sin, 14, 93, 94, 96, 111
Orwell, George, 4-5, 6, 24, 28, 33, 46, 72, 82, 86, 87, 103, 105
Owen, Robert, 108

Pallen, Condé B., 84
Parsons, Talcott, 111, 114-115, 118, 120, 126
Patrick, J. Max, 28
People of the Ruins, The (Shanks), 85
Perry, Ralph Barton, 65
Piaget, Jean, 42, 52, 56

Plato, 4, 7, 12, 16, 17, 36, 38, 59, 62, 103, 108, 109, 110, 112, 124
Pleasure, 3-4
Polak, Fred L., 26
Political Justice (Godwin), 35
Politics, utopianism and, 91-101
Popper, Karl, 28, 107, 125
"Positive reinforcement," 15
Pride, 14

Rank, Otto, 33
Reality, 20
Reason, appeal to, 65
Religions, institutionalized, 47
Republic (Plato), 109, 124
"Reversibility," 52-53
Revolt of the Pedestrians (Keller), 86
Rights of Man doctrine, 96
Rise of the Meritocracy, The (Young), 77-80
Robespierre, 127
Rogers, Carl R., 25
Roosevelt, Franklin D., 68
Rousseau, Jean Jacques, 120
R.U.R., 85, 88
Russell, Bertrand, 28

Seidenberg, Roderick, 28
Sewell, E., 56
Shanks, Edward, 84, 85
Shklar, Judith N., 28
Skinner, B. F., 12-19, 25, 57-75, 83
Smith, Winston, 84
Social system, 109-123
Social System (Parsons), 111, 116, 120, 126
Socialism, 19, 20
Sociological analysis, 103-126
Socrates, 103, 109
Stevens, Wallace, 1-3, 22, 24
Story of Utopias (Mumford), 82

Structure of Social Action (Parsons), 115
"Sunday Morning" (Stevens), 1-3, 24
Surrealists, 88
Swastika Night (Constantine), 87
Swift, Jonathan, 82

Talmon, J. L., 10, 24, 91-101
Tanner, J., 56
Technetronic Age, 127-150
Technology, 21, 23, 30, 38, 86, 95, 127-150
Thompson, J. Arthur, 33
Tolstoi, L., 30
Totalitarianism, 9, 10
Twenty-fifth Hour (Gheorghiu), 82, 83, 87

Unhappiness, 7, 8
Usher II (Bradbury), 9, 88

Valéry, Paul, 85
Variété, 85
Virtue, 11, 12, 14, 16
Voltaire, 82
Vonnegut, Kurt, 86

Wolden Two (Skinner), 12, 13, 16, 25, 70, 83, 84, 86
Walsh, Chad, 28
We, 85
Weber, Eugen, 81-89
Weber, Max, 118
Wells, H. G., 7-9, 10, 17, 24, 33, 46, 123
Whyte, Lancelot, 33
Wiener, Anthony J., 26
Williams, Donald C., 25

Young, Michael, 28, 77-80

Zamiatin, Eugene, 28, 84, 85